The Oxford Historical Pageant, June 27-July 3, 1907

Book of Words

The
Oxford Historical Pageant,

June 27—July 3, 1907

Book of Words

With Illustrations

Oxford
Printed for the Pageant Committee
1907

OXFORD: PRINTED AT THE
UNIVERSITY PRESS WITH THE
ANCIENT TYPES (Circ. 1677) OF
BISHOP FELL; BY HORACE HART,
PRINTER TO THE UNIVERSITY

PREFATORY NOTE

THE Oxford Historical Pageant consists of fifteen Scenes and an Interlude or Masque, and of these sixteen parts nine are dramatic scenes with words, and the rest spectacular only. The present Book of Words contains (1) the nine dramatic scenes in full, with marks [1] to show what parts, from considerations of time, will be omitted in the performance; (2) a description of the spectacular scenes; and (3) short links connecting the successive parts. It will be readily understood that there has been great difficulty in selecting what incidents in the long and varied history of the City and University would best fit in with the necessary limitations of a Pageant.

The Pageant Committee have been exceptionally fortunate in securing the generous help of Mr. Laurence Housman, Mr. Robert Bridges, Mr. Laurence Binyon, Professor Oman, Mr. A. D. Godley, Professor Walter

---

[1] A wavy line in the margin.

Raleigh, Mr. James B. Fagan, Miss Wordsworth, and
Mr. Stanley Weyman for the present volume. Mr. Robert
Bridges has also contributed an 'Invitation to the Pageant',
and Mr. A. T. Quiller Couch a characteristic Epilogue on
'The Secret of Oxford'. Mr. J. Wells has kindly supplied
the links. To all these helpers the Committee tender their
sincere thanks, and feel that they are making a poor return
for such brilliant services. The Consultative Committee
has also ungrudgingly undertaken the editing of this
volume[1] and the selection of the illustrations: while to
Mr. Falconer Madan and Professor Oman, who have per-
sonally revised the proofs and given unsparingly of their
time and energy, the gratitude of all concerned is pre-
eminently due.

It is perhaps advisable to point out that a modern
Pageant, like an historical play of Shakespeare, is often
compelled, by reasons of space, time, and suitability for
representation, to foreshorten history. The critic must
not murmur if persons and events are found in a juxta-
position for which there is no absolute warrant in the
chronicles, or if fancy sometimes bodies forth possibilities
which may never have been realities.

Grateful acknowledgement is due to the Delegates of
the Clarendon Press for allowing use to be made of some

---

[1] With the exception of the Appendix.

Oxford Almanack plates and of the illustrated Catalogues of the Historical Portraits Exhibitions of 1904, 1905, and 1906; to the Society of Antiquaries of London for permission to reproduce a plate from *Archæologia*, vol. liii; to the Oxford Historical Society and to Messrs. James Parker and Son, of Oxford for similar indulgences [1]; and to Mr. C. Davis, of 2 Cornmarket Street, Oxford, for permission to reproduce on Pl. III a scene from the Frideswide Window at Christ Church. The volume is published on May 25, 1907.

[1] Plates II and VIII respectively.

LIST OF CONTENTS

LIST OF ILLUSTRATIONS

AN

INVITATION TO THE PAGEANT

ODE BY ROBERT BRIDGES

FAIR lady of learning, playfellow of spring,
 Who to thy towery hospice in the vale
 Invitest all, with queenly claim to bring
Scholars from every land within thy pale;
If aught our pageantry may now avail
To paint thine antique story to the eye,
Inspire the scene, and bid thy herald cry
 Welcome to all, and to all comers hail!

Come hither, then he crieth, and hail to all:
 Bow each his heart a pilgrim at her shrine,
Whatever chance hath led you to my call,
 Ye that love pomp, and ye that seek a sign,
 Or on the low earth look for things divine;
Nor ye, whom reverend Camus near-allied,
Writes in the roll of his ennobled pride,
 Refrain your praise and love to mix with mine.

Praise her, the mother of celestial moods,
 Who o'er the saints' inviolate array
Hath starr'd her robe of fair beatitudes
 With jewels worn by Hellas, on the day
 She grew from girlhood into wisdom gay;
And hath laid by her crozier, ever more
With both hands gathering to enrich her store,
 And make her courts with music ring alway.

Love her, for that the world is in her heart,
 Man's rude antiquity and doubtful goal,
The heaven-enthralling luxury of art,
 The burden'd pleading of his clay-bound soul,

The mutual office of delight and dole,
The merry laugh of youth, the joy of life
Older than thought, and the unamending strife
    Twixt liberty and politic control.

There is none holier, not the lilied town
    By Arno, whither the spirit of Athens fled,
Escap't from Hades to a less renown,
    Yet joyful to be risen from the dead;
    Nor she whose wide imperious arms were spread
To spoil mankind, until the avenger came
In darkening storm, and left a ruin'd name,
    A triple crown upon a vanquish't head.

What love in myriad hearts in every clime
    The vision of her beauty 'calls to pray'r:
Where at his feet Himâlaya sublime
    Holds up aslope the Arabian floods, or where
    Patriarchal Nile rears at his watery stair;
In the broad islands of the Antipodes,
By Esperanza, or in the coral seas
    Where Buddha's vain pagodas throng the air;

Or where the chivalry of Nipon smote
    The wily Muscovite, intent to creep
Around the world with half his pride afloat,
    And sent his battle to the soundless deep;
    Or with our pilgrim-kin, and them that reap
The prairie-corn beyond cold Labrador
To California and the Alaskan shore,
    Her exiled sons their pious memory keep:

Bright memories of young poetic pleasure
    In free companionship, the loving stress
Of all life-beauty lull'd in studious leisure,
    When every Muse was jocund with excess

Of fine delight and tremulous happiness:
The breath of an indolent unbridled June,
When delicate thought fell from the dreamy moon:
  But now strange care, sorrow and grief oppress.

'*Ah! fewer tears shall be,*—'tis thus they dream,—
  Ah, fewer, softer tears, when we lie low:
On younger brows shall brighter laurel gleam:
  Lovelier and earlier shall the rosebuds blow.'
For in this hope she nurs'd them, and to know
That Truth, while men regard a tetter'd page,
Leaps on the mountains, and from age to age
  Reveals the dayspring's inexhausted glow.

Yet all their joy is mingled with regret:
  As the lone scholar on a neighbouring height,
Brooding disconsolate with eyelids wet
  Ere o'er the unkind world he took his flight,
  Look'd down upon her festal lamps at night,
And while the far call of her warning bell
Reach't to his heart, sang us his fond farewell,
  Beneath the stars thinking of lost delight;

'Farewell! for whether we be young or old,
  Thou dost remain, but we shall pass away;
Time shall against himself thy house uphold,
  And build thy sanctuary from decay;
  Children unborn shall be thy pride and stay.
May Earth protect thee, and thy sons be true,
And God with heavenly food thy life renew,
  Thy pleasure and thy grace from day to day.'

PLATE II

SEAL OF ST. FRIDESWIDE'S PRIORY, A.D. 1291

Enlarged from a Durham Roll.

The legend is Sigillum Ecclesie Sancte Frideswide Oxoniensis. St. Frideswide is depicted beneath a canopy
with a flower in one hand and an open book in the other. From an illustration in *Collectanea*, vol. II
(Oxf. Hist. Soc.).

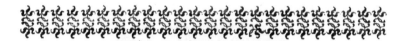

SAINT FRIDESWIDE

(THE BEGINNINGS OF THE CITY)

Circa A.D. 727

In the centre a wattled hut. A sound of sheep-bells is heard, and from among the trees a boy's voice singing.

BOY.

HEAR ye, hear ye!
　　Far away and near ye,
　　　　The cuckoo,
　　　　The cuckoo,
The cuckoo by his lone self a-singing.
　　　Say true, cuckoo,
　Whither away art thou winging?

Round the shore of the island a small fishing-boat is poled leisurely toward the landing-place. As the song ends two fishermen land, and begin unloading a great pile of nets.

FISHERMEN. Ahoy! Ahoy! Ahoy!

From the hut comes a peasant, followed by his wife who stands in the doorway holding a child in her arms. From under the trees come three or four young shepherds, who move toward the landing-stage: the BOY with a pipe slung at his neck follows indolently with the idle call of 'cuckoo' still on his lips. The nets are landed and stretched out along the grass or slung up on stakes by the side of the hut to dry. As one of the fishermen returns to the boat, he stands startled and points up stream. A boat is seen approaching fast, with four rowers, and bearing FRIDESWIDE *and her maidens. In the stern stands an old servitor who gazes anxiously to the rear. The shepherds gather to watch: the fishermen wade into the stream and draw the boat to shore.* FRIDESWIDE *lands by the aid thus proffered: her*

B

maidens follow. The boat is moored; peasants and shepherds
stand at a respectful distance and look on with curiosity.

FRIDES.   Here the smooth shore invites our feet to land.
      Hither, my maidens, and, on either hand,
      Give hands to guide me!
                  [She advances, supported by her maidens;
                       presently her feet fail.
                    Nay! for I am spent
      With flight and fasting!
1ST MAID.   Here, then, rest content!
2ND MAID. Lady, lie here and sleep! And may the girth
      Of this broad heaven, and this all green earth,
      Fold thee to peace!
FRIDES.   See that none follows nigh
      Of those we fear!
                [Two of her male attendants go down to
                   the river bank to keep watch.
             O sweet Earth, let me lie
      In safety on thy breast by this green wood!
      But thou [*to an attendant*], go swift, and seek that Sister-
         hood
      Which near this place hath made a home of prayer
      And poverty! Commend me to their care,
      And bid them here to help me in my great need.

The attendant goes, led by the BOY *who shows him the way. The*
old servitor meanwhile has been in colloquy with the peasant
whose wife has moved him to offer the shelter of their home.

OLD SERV. Lady, here comes unlooked-for help indeed—
      Yon herdsman's hut: for sure so low a roof
      To guard so high a head gives likelier proof
      Of safety than can these poor hands of age.
      Here shalt thou hide, and when thy foeman's rage
      Hath borne him by, then shall our path lie clear.
FRIDES.   Be it as thou wilt. And yet, I fear, I fear!
            [She enters the hut with her maidens.

PEASANT. What is this fear?

OLD SERV.　　　　　　　　Of one, Algar by name,
　　　　Who, shameless, seeks to do our mistress shame.
　　　　But she to Heaven is vowed; and he, set sore
　　　　To his dark purpose, came with threat of war
　　　　Against our King, her father. From which dread
　　　　In secret haste the Princess Frideswide fled—
　　　　Not willing on her kinsfolk to bring doom.
　　　　But he—swift to pursue—Prince Algar, whom
　　　　None dares withstand, now follows fierce and fain.
　　　　And, since no speed avails, we seek to gain
　　　　In lowly hiding cover from the cast
　　　　Of his quick nets.

ROWER. [*Comes running*]　　Master, here cometh fast
　　　　Down stream a warship! black it breasts the tide;
　　　　And lo, hard after, follows one beside
　　　　Like to it, hemming us on either hand
　　　　With threat of onslaught. Look! They land, they land!

*While he speaks two large galleys are to be seen approaching, full of
　　armed men: they divide to right and left and land their forces
　　on both shores. ALGAR and his men leap to shore and rush
　　forward shouting their war-cry.*

ALL.　　Algar! Algar! Ho! Ho! To the Hunt! Algar!

*The fishermen fall back dismayed. FRIDESWIDE's followers are over-
　　thrown and made prisoners. ALGAR comes forward, recognizes
　　the old servitor and points his men toward the hut. They
　　rush in; a cry of women is heard. FRIDESWIDE and her
　　maidens are haled forth. FRIDESWIDE alone shows no terror
　　as she is led forward to where ALGAR awaits her. Her
　　captors loose her and stand round, cutting off all means of
　　escape.*

ALGAR.　So, Frideswide, we stand face to face again!
　　　　And thy dark flight and devious ways were vain

To foil me from the prize. Now hast thou found
The master of thy fate. Nay, look not round
For help of gods or men. The heavens are dumb
To thy dumb prayer So yield thyself, and come!

He reaches out his hand to seize her. FRIDESWIDE *starts back, making
the sign of the Cross against him with outstretched arms.*

FRIDES. Oh, ye strong powers of Heaven, unseen yet nigh,
Now to my prayer give ear! Help, when I cry!

Thunder is heard, and a flash of light is seen falling upon ALGAR.
*He staggers, throws up his hands with a cry, and covers his
face. All shrink away from him in horror; as the circle widens
he stretches out his hands helplessly for aid.*

ALGAR. Ah me! what horror of death, and doom,—what night
Hath stept between my vision and the light?
Oh, friends! Oh, comrades, reach a hand to me!

RETAINER. What, what means this? Those eyes on vacancy
Stare wide! He's blind!

ALL. Blind!

SEVERAL. The wrath of God hath smitten him; he is blind.

ALGAR. Oh, will no friend reach me his hand to guide?

All draw back except FRIDESWIDE. *While two of her maidens seek
fearfully to restrain her, she advances and takes* ALGAR *by the
hand.*

FRIDES. Here's mine.

ALGAR.   Who is it? Who?

FRIDES.   'Tis I—Frideswide.

ALGAR. Frideswide! Thou hand of God. Smite and I die!
O heart of charity, if prayer may lie
On lips so pure for one so stained and foul,
Pray thou for me Heaven's pardon on my soul!

He kneels at FRIDESWIDE'S *feet and holds the hem of her robe. As*
FRIDESWIDE *stands and prays all kneel or bow.*

FRIDES. O Thou, that art the source of light,
Who givest unto mortals sight,

PLATE III

ALGAR STRUCK BLIND

A scene from the life of St. Frideswide, as depicted in the East Window of the Latin Chapel
at the Cathedral, designed by Burne Jones and executed by William Morris.

Filling all Nature to the brim
With liquid life, pour light on him
Whose feet till now have walked in night,
So henceforth shall he see aright.

ALL. Oh, look! She lifts him from his knees!
His eyes are healed. He sees, he sees!

ALGAR. O tree and field, and blessed earth,
And running river, and fair sky,
How shall my word proclaim her worth
Who gives me eyes to see you by?
Ah, saintly maiden, though my speech be rude,
My heart is ripe to prove its gratitude,
Let but the way be shown!

Enter TWELVE NUNS *who advance towards* FRIDESWIDE *bearing the
robe and veil and pastoral staff of an Abbess.*

FRIDES.   Lo, yonder come
Those in whose midst I seek to make my home.
Provide the means: and I for these will build
A house of rest, that here, with prayer fulfilled,
Our lives may give fresh strength to all around.
For, lo, this space of fields is holy ground,
Chosen of God.

The NUNS *approach and invest* FRIDESWIDE *with the symbols of
authority;* ALGAR *takes off his jewels and crown and lays them
as offerings upon his shield borne on spears. A cart drawn by
a yoke of oxen is led forward and made ready to convey* FRIDE-
SWIDE *to her destination.*

FRIDES. Soon from yon river, wound about her roots,
A tree of life shall rise with healing fruits
For all the nations; and her blood shall be
Warm in a race that spreads from sea to sea.
And here a town shall spring, with spire and dome,
And these broad meadows shall become the home
Of learning; and the wonder of man's mind

Fixed for all future ages here enshrined
Shall have safe dwelling; and by these fair streams
Old men see visions, and young men dream dreams.
So, shall all Time behold the light shed wide,
Of Wisdom, in her children justified!

ALGAR *makes humble obeisance to* FRIDESWIDE; *led by the* NUNS
*and followed by her maidens she mounts the ox-cart; a
procession is formed; while the procession moves off, all join
in; and the boats with* ALGAR *and his retainers pass away
up stream. As the procession goes all sing:—*

CHORUS

A Daughter of Kings we here behold,
Whose glory clings like a robe of gold;
And the gifts that she brings are manifold.

With gladness of sound shall she be brought;
For here we have found whom long we sought,
With virtue around her as raiment wrought.

Instead of fathers thou shalt have sons,
And thy house be the home of the mighty ones,
Whose fame shall endure while all time runs.

For out of thee a city shall rise,
Whose walls shall be as light to the eyes,
A strength for the free, and a rest to the wise

LAURENCE HOUSMAN.

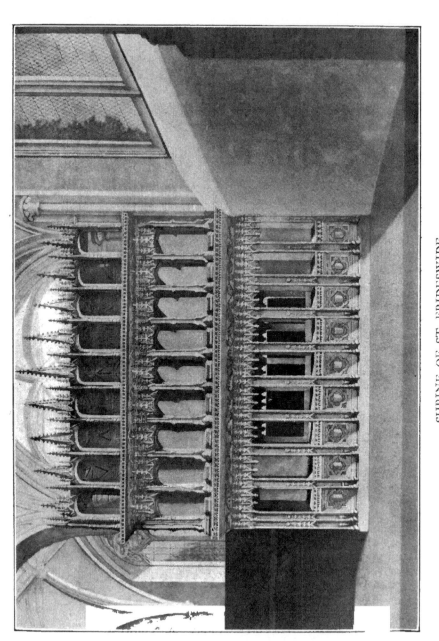

SHRINE OF ST. FRIDESWIDE.

THE story of Oxford begins with the legend of St. Frideswide in the eighth century; its history begins two hundred years later with the brief mention of the Chronicle that King Edward, the first of that name, took into his own hands 'Lundenbyrg' and 'Oxnaford' and all the lands that were obedient thereto. It was already an important city, as its conjunction with London shows; hence it played an important part in the troubles with the Danes, and it was the scene of the coronation of one of our three Danish kings.

0

CORONATION OF KING HAROLD II

From the Bayeux Tapestry.

THE CORONATION
OF HAROLD HAREFOOT

A. D. 1036—7

THE scene opens with the entrance of choir and Benedictine
monks, upon one side, and with the approach of the Court,
including the King's Mother, Elgiva of Northampton, and
the Queen Consort, upon the other; amongst the ladies are Godiva,
wife of Earl Leofric, and Elfleda, wife of Earl Siward.

Then enters the ecclesiastical procession. It is headed by the
Cross, flanked by four lights, two borne upon each side; the Cross
is immediately followed by incense-bearers, swinging censers;
behind these, again, come deacons in tunicles and priests in chasubles.
Two Bishops carrying their crosiers and preceded by lights, come
next in order, and after them walk the deacons in attendance on
the Archbishop, Elfric of York[1], one bearing the ampulla of oil, the
other the Gospel-book. Finally, with other lights carried before
him, comes the Archbishop himself, holding his crosier like his
brother Bishops.

A sound of cheering is heard without, and the King's procession approaches. Before the royal person are borne, first the
ring, then the sword, then the crown, then the sceptre and virge,
and lastly the pallium and tunic: thirty warriors, headed by the
great Earls, Leofric of Mercia and Siward of Northumbria, raise
Harold upon a broad shield. The shield is lowered to the ground
behind the throne and the King descends, while the first coronation
chant begins. Two Bishops take their Sovereign by the hands and
lead him to the platform, on which the Archbishop now mounts,

---

[1] Ethelnoth, Archbishop of Canterbury, had refused to officiate, being a
partisan of Harold's brother and rival, Harthacnut.

followed by the monarch.   Elfric then, taking Harold's hand, leads him to each of the four sides of the platform, beginning at the north, continuing with the west and south, and ending with the east, and solemnly presents him to his people on the four quarters of the heaven.   Shouts of *Hail* greet him from each side: the royal largesse follows.

The Archbishop then goes up to the altar, followed by his deacons; next come the two Bishops, leading the King, as before, one by each hand.   Harold kneels upon the altar-step, and now the first coronation chant is ended.

The King next rises, turns to the people, and makes his formal promise of good government.   As he kneels again, the second chant (*Zadok the Priest*) commences, and the ceremonial of the coronation proper is performed.   First comes the unction ('Not all the water in the rough rude sea Can wash the balm off from an anointed king'); next the ring and tunic are put on; the King is then girt with the sword and vested with the pallium; lastly, the crown is put upon his head, the sceptre in his right hand, the virge in his left, and the Sovereign, whose election has been thus completely ratified with every formality, is led back to the throne-platform by the two Bishops, and placed upon the throne amid the acclamations of all around.

The King and his warriors themselves head the departure of the royal procession, followed by the courtiers, earls, Queen, maids of honour, &c.   The choir and monks are the last to leave.

THE days of universities were not yet, but there were students before there were universities. These gathered especially in the great towns, where life was full of interest and where charity was abundant. Oxford had suffered from the Norman Conquest, and Domesday Book tells a sad story of 'waste' houses; but its prosperity returned when Robert D'Oilgi, its castle-builder, turned saint and church-builder, and to this reviving and prosperous Oxford came Theobald Stampensis, the first of its long series of teachers.

PLATE II

MASTER AND SCHOLARS

From the title-page of a Donatus Minor, entitled *Rudimenta Grammatice*, printed at Vienna
about 1495. The birch sufficiently indicates the practical nature of the instruction.

THEOBALDUS STAMPENSIS

(THE BEGINNINGS OF THE UNIVERSITY)

Circa A.D. 1110

SCENE.—A PUBLIC THOROUGHFARE. *Enter* THEOBALD OF ÉTAMPES *with his disciples.*

THEOBALD. I MUST be seen and heard. Therefore I led you
To this road, where the townsfolk mostly pass:
For they will gather to us. Close around me
To right and left: some, when they see you
    harkening,
Will stay to hear.
1ST STUDENT.   Pray you continue, Sir,
Where we left yesterday.
THEOBALD. (If there shall be a school such as I dream of
We must find scholars. See! we are yet ten—
I stand to fish; have faith that Heav'n to-day
Will send me a miraculous draught. Meanwhile
We may read Virgil.)—Look! by ill-fortune,
Three pestilential monks!

Enter MONKS.

1ST MONK.   Is not that he,
The man we spake of, who reviles our order?
Theobald of Estamps, Reasoner and Churchman?
THEOBALD. We fish not for these pike: let them pass on.
MONK. [*approaching*] Art thou not Theobald the Frenchman?

THEOBALD.   I am.

MONKS.   What doest thou here in Oxenford?—
      Meddler—
      We were well rid of thee: why cam'st thou again?—
      Why didst thou leave thy country?—

THEOBALD.   Ask of God
      Why he call'd Abram to the Promised Land.

1ST MONK.   Wilt tell us, O Blasphemer, that God taught thee
      That evil word of thine, when thou didst say
      'A monastery is a prison of the damn'd'?

THEOBALD.   And wherefore not?
        [*The citizens gather about* THEOBALD.]

MONKS.   Liar!—
      Contemptuous priest!
      Thou hast damn'd us!

THEOBALD.   I say ye damn yourselves
      Better than anybody else could damn you.

MONK.   We spake no ill of thee . . . Accursed tongue!

THEOBALD.   Ye live in idleness, distemper'd fatness,
      Darkness and ignorance.

MONKS. [*attempting to get at* THEOBALD] Some of you, help!

THEOBALD   Ye denounce the world,
      Yet nothing do to amend it.

MONKS [*prevented by citizens, who take* THEOBALD's *part.*]
      Silence him!
      Seize him!

CITIZENS.   Nay, we will hear him speak—
      —Speak on, Sir, what you will.
      —Fear not these drones!

THEOBALD.   I fear them not. Let them pass on in peace.

CITIZENS. [*driving off the* MONKS]
      Begone! Begone! or we will harry you!
      Be off to your old ridiculous Abingdon.
                [*Exeunt* MONKS.

1ST CITIZEN.   If thou'rt the Norman priest who came among us
      Some years agone, we have heard well of thee,

And wish to hear thee. Tell us first where thou hast been,
And why return'd.

THEOBALD   Now, if it is you that ask me
Wherefore I come again to you, I will answer . . .
Not without invitation of yourselves,
And the plain finger of Heav'n.—It happen'd thus . . .
In Paris, whither I had gone to study,˙I met
A fellow-student, a young clerk, a very boy,
Who draws all to him.—Truth, so he teaches,
Is not prescribable by mere authority
Of other minds, who had no other means
To find Truth than have we. We should use learning
To free the mind, not chain it: and the Truth
Will set us free.

CITIZENS. Well said, Sir.
He says well.
What is Truth?

THEOBALD. What is Truth? Truth is what the spirit desires.

CITIZENS. Speak on, Sir!

THEOBALD.   And he can make reason live:
The doctors are confuted, and all men
Hang on his words. Now I, soon as I heard him,
Was fired to follow and cast my lot with him
Among my countrymen. But when I told
My purpose to your fellow-townsman, Rupert here,
He said, 'Go not with him. France is provided.
'Leave France to Abelard (that is his name):
'Come thou with me to England; for my people
'Are eager, as thou know'st, (and so I find you),
'To hear and question. Be the Apostle (he said)
'Of England. Found thy school in Oxenford.'

CITIZENS. Well, Sir; thou mayst.—
If thou canst teach us.—
And then thou camest?

THEOBALD.   O nay! I had ne'er returned
But for a vision . . . I saw a vision . . .

CITIZENS. Tell us ! . . .
THEOBALD. That night I dream'd.
CITIZENS. What saw'st thou ?
THEOBALD. Methought I look'd down on a lovely city
   In a wide vale : high in the South the Sun
   Smote on her crowded pinnacles, that rose
   With spiry delicacy of silver-grey,
   As 'twere a fretted casket of man's thought,
   Severe mid the soft wilderness of green.
   Beneath her walls a river flow'd, meandering
   Thro' flowery meads, rushes, and willowbanks,
   Where the sweet birds of the stream warbled all day.
   But evermore my wandering eye return'd
   Unto the lovely city—and while I look'd
   I saw a marvel: the city changed: where late
   Two towers had been were three: the low-tiled roofs
   Melted before my eyes and grew again
   In battlemented walls and chapels fair.
    And I might see what passed within the walls,
   And how the doors were throng'd with beardless boys
   And long-robed scholars : and therein awhile
   'Twas happy and peaceful, but anon outburst
   Confused riot, and fighting in the streets.
    Many the scenes I saw of future time
   Like to the pictur'd past—Now, in the halls
   Was high dispute of learning, loud the assembly
   Of purple, silk, and fur, murmur'd like bees ;
   Or hush'd to some grave doctor, who outsoar'd
   Their congregated thought. . . . 'Twas gone. Behold
   A man of innocent mien led out alone
   Beyond the walls, chain'd on a horrid pyre,
   And burn'd alive before the shuddering crowd.
   . . . Then saw I a haughty King, who with his court
   Had taken refuge, and held festival
   Within the garrison'd walls,—but all around
   His foes lay camp'd ; and full soon he was fled.

And now great domes had risen,
And churches unlike ours: and all the river
Was gay with banners flying, and painted boats.
But far into the fields the city had spread: .
The poplar groves were fell'd, and half the green
'Neath her red skirts was blotted out. . . . Whereat
Wondering, and fearing more, I saw the last
And strangest scene of all . . . I saw . .

CITIZENS. Aye! Aye!

THEOBALD. How shall I tell? Will you believe?

CITIZENS. Yea! Yea! Speak on.
What saw you?

THEOBALD I saw a man, standing where now I stand,
Clad in the selfsame robe that now I wear,
Speaking as I speak, and unto you; for ye
Stood round me then in that far time as now.
Myself I saw . . .

CITIZENS.   Go on, Sir! Say, what next!

THEOBALD. Your words amaze me. 'Tis my dream again.

CITIZENS. What follow'd then?
What is to come?

THEOBALD. Around, behind you a vast crowd was gather'd,
Sitting as men sit in a theatre
To see a play: and here my image stood
Before that multitude of gazing eyes
And ears that harken'd to me; and when I ceased
The people cheer'd.

CITIZENS. [cheering]
I will learn of thee, Sir!
And I . . . And I . . .
Where is thy Hall?
To the city! To the city!
Lead on!

THEOBALD. Come. Follow me I am your leader. To-day
We lay foundations of a school to make
This city glorious. Long, too long hath been

c

The night of ignorance, the age of darkness;
Now is the dawn of learning. Ecce iam noctis . . .
1st Citizen. [*singing*] Ecce iam noctis . . .

All in chorus singing

Ecce iam noctis tenuatur umbra!
Lucis Aurora rutilans coruscat!
Viribus totis rogitemus omnes
Omnipotentem.

Exeunt omnes.

Robert Bridges.

PLATE VII

GREEK HALL

A favourable specimen of an academical hall, representing the intermediate stage of develop-
ment between the earliest unorganized condition and the College system. Only one (St. Edmund
Hall) still maintains a separate and precarious existence. Greek Hall was near St. John's
College, and the original view is in the Bodleian.

THE students at Oxford had other patrons than the citizens. Henry I, and still more his greater namesake Henry II, were both lovers of learning and learned men; whether it was for this reason that the first Henry had his palace, Beaumont, at Oxford it is impossible to say. Certain it is that during the twelfth century the mention of teachers and of students in Oxford become more and more frequent, and it may well be true that the University as an organized body was founded by a migration of English scholars from the schools of Paris to those of Oxford (about 1167), caused by the king's quarrel with his archbishop.

PLATE VII

CHARTER OF KING JOHN TO OXFORD

A facsimile of the earliest original Charter in the possession of the City of Oxford, dated June 14, 1199. It confirms the previous charters of Henry II, granting the Vill of Oxford to the burghers. The first words are 'Johannes Dei gratia Rex Angliæ, Dominus Hiberniæ'. It is on parchment, with a fragment of the Great Seal still appendant.

HENRY II
AND FAIR ROSAMUND

At the opening of the scene ROSAMUND CLIFFORD *stands alone on the
river bank; under the bank is a boat waiting, with a boatman;
on the further shore nuns are passing slowly in procession.*

ROSAMUND, *as she speaks, turns now to the nuns, with outstretched
arms, now to the flowers which she holds in her hands and which
she drops, one by one.*

ROSAMUND.   I COME to you; I come. One moment more,
              And then I come.—Now must you fall and wither,
              Flowers! When I smell your sweetness, all swims
                  back
          That must for ever be forgotten. Ah,
          Not on these banks you grew, but in my heart,
          You lost ones—this a song, and that a kiss—
          And where you each were plucked, there's a wound here.
                              [*Pressing her hand on her breast.*
          Wait for me, gracious sisters! O to be
          Purified and enfortressed in your prayers!
          I am afraid, because my sins were sweet.
          Now where remembrance feasted, it must fast.
          Dear blossoms, Rosamund's lost coronal,
          Fall and farewell!

During this speech HENRY *and* BECKET *have ridden on to the scene.*
HENRY, *seeing* ROSAMUND, *dismounts hurriedly and cries out*

HENRY.   Rosamund! Rosamund!
          Flown from your bower, my bird? Up and away
          To Woodstock, to our close nest in the leaves!

There's peril when your beauty goes abroad
What do you here, madcap, with the sweet eyes
That make the blood dance in my heart? To-day
Love must go hide, since kings are leisureless.

[*Advancing nearer.*

Ah, Rosamund! So dumb? so pale? so cold?

BECKET   [*Pointing to a litter and procession approaching some way off*]
                  The Queen!

HENRY.   Peace, Thomas.—Wait me, Rosamund,
At Woodstock in the bower; speed quickly there
Till Henry comes.

ROSAMUND.   Farewell—farewell for ever!
The secret's found, the clue is stolen, the bower
Is broken down, is empty and desolate. Ay,
Rosamund is shamed, Rosamund lives no more
Forget her!

HENRY.   Eleanor did this! By heaven,
But I'll avenge it: I will mew her hate
In prison doors—

ROSAMUND   Hate cannot hurt me now.
I go to Godstow, there to be received
Of yonder nuns within their holy walls,
Where I must pray to be washed clean of soil
By penitence and vigil. See, they wait me

BECKET.   She chooses well. Peace rest upon her choice

HENRY.   What, thou, my rose, my red rose of the world,
To fast and fade within a stony cell!
Impossible!

The QUEEN's *procession has now drawn close, and the* QUEEN *from
her litter glares angrily at* ROSAMUND.
Meanwhile from the other side the MAYOR *and* CITIZENS *of Oxford
have approached.*

BECKET.   The Queen is here.

HENRY. [*turning angrily*]   The Queen!
By this anointed head, she shall repent.

BECKET. The citizens of Oxford!
ROSAMUND.   Now, farewell.

During the ensuing scene she descends into the boat, which slowly
   rows away.

As HENRY *pauses between the groups the boy* RICHARD *runs up to*
   him.

HENRY. [*to Richard*] What is it, boy? Well, have it then,
         my Richard.

                    [*Giving him a dagger from his belt.*

THE MAYOR. Welcome from Oxford to our King and Queen!
         Humbly we bend our knees to our liege lord
         And pray the charter of our privileges
         Be now confirmed, as is our loyalty.
HENRY. Mayor of Oxford, and her citizens,
         You know this City holds a special seat
         In our affection; for I love her streams
         Where I have idly fished, I love the trees
         That border their clear waters; hawk on wrist,
         I have ridden on your hills and seen how fair
         Is Oxford, moated from her enemies:
         But most because our Richard, this my boy,
         Is Oxford's child and in yon palace walls
         First drew the air.—Give me the charter, Becket.
         Here are your rights renewed, nothing retrenched,
         Your liberties and contracts reaffirmed
         To trade in our dominions without let—
         Hold and use faithfully! Who breaks our bond
         Shall suffer.
THE MAYOR.   Gracious is your majesty,
         Most royal in your grace; we will requite it
         With service of our utmost faculty.
         Heaven prosper England's King and all his line!

The CITIZENS *move off in procession,* **with** *the* QUEEN **and** *her* ATTENDANTS.

BECKET.　So is your throne well buttressed.

HENRY. [*laughing*]　　　　　　　　　　Surer so
　　　Than by my barons' lances?　Now—

BECKET.　　　　　　　　　　　　　Look yonder!

HENRY *turns and sees* ROSAMUND *in the boat already arriving at the other shore; she looks round once, then goes forward to the waiting nuns.*

HENRY.　Rosamund! 's death! Gone from me! Now indeed
　　　This Queen of mine shall sup on what she brewed,
　　　And kneel, and weep, and find her hate strike home
　　　More pitiless than she.　To horse! Away!

　　　　　　[HENRY *and* BECKET *throw themselves on their horses and ride off.*

　　　　　　　　　　　　　LAURENCE BINYON.

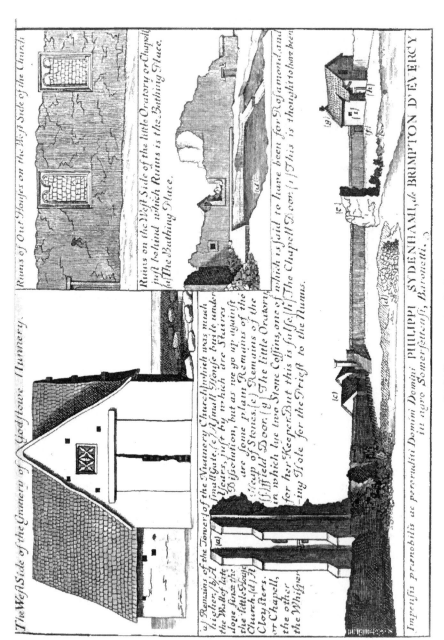

The West Side of the Nunnery of Godstow Nunnery.

Ruins of Out Houses on the West Side of the Church

Ruins on the West Side of the little Oratory or Chapell just behind which Ruins is the Bathing Place. (h) The Bathing Place.

(a) Remains of the Tower of the Nunnery Church which was much higher, (b) A small Gate, (c) A small House built under the Wall of late Years, just by which are Stairs done since the Dissolution, but as we go up against the little Gate Church, (d) (e) some plain Remains of the Cloysters, (e) Remains of the (f) field Door, (g) The little Oratory or Chapell, in which lye two Stone Coffins, one of which is said to have been for Rosamond, and the other for her Keeper: But this is false, (i) The Chapell Door; (i) This is thought to have been the Whispering Hole for the Priest to the Nuns.

Impensis prænobilis ac pervenusti Domini Domini PHILIPPI SYDENHAMI, de BRIMPTON D'EVERCY in agro Somersetensi, Baronetti.

RUINS OF GODSTOW

THE University was an organized body in the reign of King
John, for its Chancellor is mentioned in 1214, and it receives
at this time certain definite privileges. At once it became the great
centre in England of the revival of learning, which was inspired
by the teaching of Saints Francis and Dominic. The friars settled
in Oxford about 1221. The Franciscan scholars were especially
famous, and their convent was 'the centre of a great educational
organization which extended throughout the land' and even to
the Continent. It was a thirteenth-century 'University Extension
Movement'. And, as always, successful teaching went hand in
hand with the advancement of knowledge. One Oxford man,
the 'Subtle Doctor' Duns Scotus, was at the head of European
scholasticism; another Oxford doctor, Roger Bacon, was so far
ahead of his own time in the province of physical research that
he was treated as a magician and imprisoned.

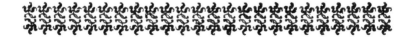

PLATE X

BACON'S STUDY

This curious gateway and chamber stood on Folly Bridge 'or Grand Pont, on the south side of Oxford, and is the traditional scene of the scientific labours of Roger Bacon.

FRIAR BACON

OR 'THERE'S NOTHING NEW UNDER THE SUN'

Circa A.D. 1271

SCENE:—AN OPEN SPACE NEAR OXFORD.

Enter (R.) CHRISTOPHER BOSSOM, *an old man with a fishing-rod of primitive type and a creel, as if bent on fishing in the river: to him (L.)* GILES BOFFIN, *a portly citizen in a hurry.*

BOSSOM. GOOD neighbour Boffin, why this eager haste?
    BOFFIN. Have you not heard? Our mighty
        conjurer,
Great Roger Bacon, has announced his purpose
Of showing all his new-invented marvels,
Here in this meadow, to the public eye,
In honour of his latest visitor,
One Master Polo, a Venetian.

While BOFFIN *is speaking enter (L.) a confused crowd headed by small boys and idlers cheering: in the rear* FRIAR BACON *and* NICOLO POLO, *a tall melancholy man, with a strange hat of oriental type.*[1] *Behind them two or three lay brothers, pushing a nondescript-looking vehicle covered with sacking, and loaded with two large parcels also swathed in coverings. The crowd forms into a semicircle, exhibiting high interest.*

POLO. Well—we have seen your famed laboratory,
    The pipes that gurgle and the spouts that hiss,
    The furnaces with crucibles aglow,

---

[1] Not the better-known traveller Marco Polo, who was a mere lad in 1271, but his father Nicolo, who was just returned from his first oriental voyage. Bacon was back in England by 1268, after his long captivity in Paris.

The jars, with many coloured labels, ranged
Much like enshielded knights in battle line,
And, wrapping all, that dense mephitic smell
That Science sheds around her votaries.
'Twas vastly pretty, and it far surpassed
All that the sorcerers of Kublai Khan
Displayed to me in distant Cambalu.
But pardon an old merchant, when he asks
If you have got to practical results:
In short,—to use our blunt Venetian phrase—
My best of friars, is there 'money in it'?

BACON.   Italian stranger, all that you have seen
Is but the by-play of a mind engrossed
In problems of divine philosophy.
But since philosophers are badly paid,
And since research costs dear, my nimble wits
Employ their leisure in devising toys
Of practical utility, whereby
I woo the pennies from the burgher's purse.
This is the truest form of Alchemy,
For so I turn my brains to gold. As thus—

                              [*producing a box*]

You know that I have deeply pondered o'er
The problem of prolonging human life—
Witness my *Opus Majus*, section vi,
Exemplum ii,—and by prolonged research
I have produced this wondrous panacea,
Compact of drugs gathered from every shore
From Tapiobane to the Fortunate Isles.
These magic globules from this scarlet box,
Taken with careful regularity,
Bestow upon the happy purchaser
The thousand winters of Methuselah.[1]

---

[1] In the passage here quoted Bacon recommends for his panacea a mixture of pounded pearls, spermaceti, aloes, gold, Tyrian snake's flesh, &c, 'which might promote longevity to an extent hitherto unimagined.'

POLO. I fancy that I heard in far Cathay
     Of pills that promised much the same result.
     And yet the public was but half-convinced
     There's too much competition in the line.

BACON. Thou doubting Thomas! Those poor mountebanks
     Who foist on rustics pills composed of bread
     With cardamums or calomel, or what not,
     Know not the uses of Advertisement!
     But I would post by every market cross,
     And on the hoardings of the crowded street,
     Nay, in the innocent fields along the road,
     Schedules writ fair, with words of monstrous size,
     Azure, and sanguine, and bright emerald,
     Stating the merits of Friar Bacon's pills
     In terms of such persuasive eloquence
     That every passer-by *must* purchase them.
     How does that strike you?

POLO.   I have still my doubts.

BACON The public is an ass: repeat your statement
     Ten thousand times, and he'll believe and swallow.
     But I've a scheme e'en better than this first.

*The lay brothers unload from their truck the two large parcels,
which, when unrolled, prove to be the* BRAZEN HEAD *and its
pedestal. They erect them in the middle of the open space. The
crowd stand amazed.*

BACON. Behold my celebrated Brazen Head!
     It utters oracles of deepest import,
     And will, if questioned, answer every riddle
     Propounded by inquirers—

BOFFIN. [*interrupting*]   Marry, Head,
[*together*] When is a door—

BOSSOM [*interrupting*]   If a herring
     And a half cost—

BACON. [*thundering at them*] Silence, triflers!—On condition
     That first you put a penny in this slot.

POLO.   [*fumbling with his purse*]
      If I should place within the orifice
      This Luxemburg denier, a pretty piece
      Palmed on me by mine host at Abingdon,
      Would the thing work?

BACON.   Not so: the slot rejects
      All pennies made in Germany or France,
      Flanders or Scotland.

POLO.   [*putting a penny in the slot*]   Well, have then thy
      will!

                [*The* BRAZEN HEAD *begins to work. After*
                  rolling its eyes it speaks in a strange
                  metallic tone.

THE HEAD.   TIME WAS: TIME IS: TIME SHALL BE![1]

POLO.   Marvellous
      The brazen head has got a brazen voice!

BACON.   That is but natural. Now propound your question.

POLO.   Well: let us search the future. Tell me, head,
      How Oxford will be faring, let us say,
      Six hundred years and forty from this date,
      In Anno Domini one-nine-nought-seven.

HEAD.   Oxford shall flourish: to her schools shall come
      Scholars from each remotest end of earth:
      From Austral Africa: from distant lands
      Beyond the Atlantic wave: from the great isle
      Far beyond Java in the Antipodes.

POLO.   An awful prospect! If the map tells true
      The races that inhabit Africa,
      Beyond Sahara, and the lands that lie
      Southward behind the Golden Chersonese,
      Are monstrous, semi-human, many-eyed,
      Or hairy-skinned: they hop upon one leg,
      Or wear their heads beneath their shoulders, or

---

[1] This is the only recorded utterance of the Head in the 'Romance of Friar Bacon'.

Enwrap their middles with their pendent ears.[1]
Shall creatures such as that walk these quiet meads
And study logic or theology ?

HEAD.   Not so: these strangers will be proper men,
As nimble in their bodies as their wits,
Speaking good English, playing English games,
And mostly subjects of our English King.

POLO.   Oh, monstrous! Friar, your brazen head talks folly.
What! English subjects in South Africa,
Or lodged beyond the Atlantic!

HEAD.   Furthermore
I prophesy that—

                [*Here a bell rings within the head, which stops
                    abruptly.*

BACON.   Now your pennyworth
Is ended! put another in the slot.

POLO.   I will not waste my money on such trash.
The toy's ingenious, but its talk is nonsense.
No man will ever lodge a second penny
Within its jaws.

BACON.   No, no! You err, my friend.
There's profit in it. But since even this
Fails to convince you of my competence
To draw the pennies of the English public,
I will unfold my very last invention,
Which has annihilated space and time.
I have produced a marvellous machine,
A horseless chariot, fleeter than the wind—
Its pace is more than twenty miles an hour.
Mount it, and I will undertake to bear you
From here to Windsor in some fifty minutes.
Its motor-spirit is the mystic oil
Drawn from the spouting wells of Caucasus,
Which meaner souls have used to make Greek fire.

---

[1] For Polo's ideas see the lower margin of the Hereford *Mappa Mundi*, where the inhabitants of the extreme South and South-East are depicted.

Ascend this seat, and test the flying car.

> [*The lay brothers have meanwhile unwrapped*
> *the vehicle, which is clearly a mediaeval*
> *motor-car. The crowd shows intense in-*
> *terest.*

POLO. From here to Windsor in some fifty minutes!
Impossible! For even if its speed
Were what you state, it would be dangerous
To scour the roads at such a headlong pace.
One vagrant cow, one wain across the street,
And the inventor is a bag of bones,
A bleeding wreck. Bethink you of the fate
Of Simon Magus when he tried to fly.

BACON. Nay, if my skilful hand is on the wheel
There is no peril. And I have devised
This little horn
[*He sounds a horn*] which hoots before my path
To warn the rustics of my swift approach
Mount and fear not—you'll very soon discover
That the sensation is extremely pleasant
If somewhat startling.

> [*The motor commences to sputter.*

Peace, thou snorting steed!
One moment more: I place upon my nose
Those spectacles of horn to guard my eyes.
Now fare we forth! Onward to Windsor, Sir!

> [*The motor goes a few paces and comes to a dead*
> *stop.* BACON *has to dismount, and makes*
> *much business with the machine. It at*
> *last starts successfully. The crowd follows*
> *cheering, and goes off in its wake.*

C. OMAN.

FOLLY BRIDGE AND BACON'S STUDY

This view from the Oxford Almanack of 1780, taken from the spot where now the College barges are moored, shows the Bridge and Gatehouse which guarded the ancient 'Ford of Oxen,' as one approached the city from the south and south-west.

THE prosperity of the University brought it inevitably into
collision with the City. The students complained then, as
they do to-day, of extortionate prices for food and lodging, and of the
dirty and unsanitary state of the town; the townsmen complained,
no doubt with good reason, of the lawlessness of the students, and
that they abused their privileges to screen themselves in acts of
dishonesty and violence. The real reason of the quarrel was that
two independent authorities could not exist side by side in the
narrow space of mediaeval Oxford—a walled city only about a mile
long by a quarter of a mile wide. The quarrels were continually
renewed, and culminated in the great riot of St. Scholastica's Day.

MERTON COLLEGE.

Perhaps the earliest representation of the oldest regularly constituted College in Oxford, marking an important stage in the development of the University from the early teaching. From Bereblock's view made in 1566, for Queen Elizabeth's visit to Oxford.

ST. SCHOLASTICA'S DAY

(THE STRUGGLE BETWEEN TOWN AND GOWN)

A.D. 1354

OUTSIDE 'SWYNDLESTOCKE', A TAVERN.

TWO SCHOLARS, *drinking*: THE HOSTESS: A DRAWER.

1ST SCH. AY, let the Stoics chide us as they can,
             Old Walter Map is still the wiser man.
[*sings*]   '*Meum est propositum in taberna mori :*
             Vinum sit oppositum morientis ori :
             Ut dicant cum venerint angelorum chorii,
             Deus sit propitius huic potatori!'

2ND SCH. Drinking to die is one thing, good my brother :
       But die of wine that's poison! that's another.
       [*To* DRAWER] Whence comes this wine, thou very
            naughty knave?

DRAWER. Marry, I know not: 'tis the best we have.

2ND SCH. Thou lying varlet! cease thy jibes and japes,
       And bring us liquor that is made of grapes!

DRAWER. Aye, so ye pay me, as ye have not yet—

2ND SCH. Marry, I'll pay thee—Thus I quit thy debt.
                   [*Breaks his head with a flagon.*

DRAWER. Oh, I am slain!   [*Falls.*

HOSTESS. Help, help! We are undone!

Enter a PROCTOR.

       O master Proctor, they have slain my son!

PROCTOR. What means this uproar?

1ST SCH. Nay, 'tis nothing but
       A crown that's cracked—*confregit occiput.*

PROCTOR. Woman, the Chancellor his Court will see
    Thy wrongs are righted.
HOSTESS. Nay, no courts for me: *[Exit crying.*
    Help, townsmen, help!

        [Noise outside, cries of 'Town, Town!'

PROCTOR. [*to Scholars*]
    Ye silly roistering crew,
    Meseems your folly ye are like to rue.
    E'en now their clamour all the city fills:

       [Cry of 'Slay, Slay!' 'Bills and Bows!'

    Hark! Bills and bows!
1ST SCH. I'll warrant them for 'bills'.
PROCTOR. [*to Scholars*]
    Back to your halls, else to your cost ye'll hear on't!

*Enter a mob of citizens, carrying a black flag: from the other
side, a MASTER OF ARTS, with his Scholars.*

M A. [*to* PROCTOR]
    Magister, *quare gentes fremuerunt?*
A CITIZEN. These murderous Scholars, spawn of hated race,
    Who kill our townsmen in their dwelling-place—
M.A. *Negatur Major.* I herein espy
    A plain Petitio Principii.
    Hast thou not read what Seneca hath writ
    Concerning anger?
CITIZEN. Nay, nor care a whit.
    I do defy thy necromantic Latin:
    We'll sack your halls, and burn the Schools ye sat in!
    Have at them, comrades!
2ND CIT. Give good knocks!
3RD CIT. Slay, Slay!
M.A Nay, that's a game that more than one can play.

       *[They fight: great noise and disorder: Citizens
         drive out nearly all Scholars.*

PLATE XIII

KING AND CHANCELLOR, A.D. 1375

Edward III is depicted granting a charter of privileges to the Chancellor of the University:
the latter, in tri-lined gown and tippet of miniver, is kneeling. The original is in the
oldest Vice-Chancellor's Statute Book, known as 'A'.

1ST SCH. These be wild doings. Would I could but win
To Balliol College, from this horrid din!

[Enter more Scholars.

1ST SCH. Whence, whither fly ye?
2ND SCH. Sooth, I know not, I:
Only I know, that who would live must fly.
No hope of safety in Oxonia's walls:
They slay our Scholars and they rob our halls:
O doleful day! when learning lies o'erthrown,
Nor Alma Mater can protect her own!

[Enter a mob of armed citizens.

1ST SCH. Od's life, these imps of Satan come again!
Stand fast, good scholars, or we shall be slain.

*[Ecclesiastical Procession. A scholar takes refuge
with the procession but is dragged away and
killed.*

Men run across the stage, shouting 'The Chancellor!'

Enter the CHANCELLOR, *with an armed guard, with crowd.*

CHANCELLOR. Lead in these men, whose caitiff following
Is by the favour of our lord the King
Given to our hands.

Enter MAYOR *and* ALDERMEN, *guarded.*

How now, ye rascal crew,
Whose deeds outrageous call for vengeance due,
What can ye say?
MAYOR. Most noble Chancellor,
Our heinous acts we do hereby abhor:
Suppliants we come in penance for our guilt:
We are thy slaves to deal with as thou wilt.
CHANCELLOR. Ill-ordered citizens, whose horrid rout
Hath scared our Muses from their Castaly,
Hear now the doom whereof our gracious Prince
Hath made me utterer:—First, ye shall arraign

Those malefactors who their murderous hands
Have in our streets with innocent blood imbrued:
Next, on this day in each succeeding year,
This luckless day of St. Scholastica,
E'en in this place, before St. Mary's Church,
Ye shall, in memory of these wicked acts,
With proffered tribute and with haltered necks
In humble fear submit yourselves unto
The rulers of our Academic State.

MAYOR. We do accept our sovereign lord's behest.

CHANCELLOR. The doom is spoken.—May your lives, I pray,
Show due remembrance of this direful day;
And 'twixt the Muses' and your own domain
Let peace and harmony for ever reign!

[*Exeunt omnes.*

MONKS *cross stage singing*

Qui in cruce pependisti,
Qui salutem promisisti,
Arceantur hostes isti!
  Spes est nostra penes Te!
Ope salva nos divina,
Vis sit procul et rapina,
Absque morte repentina
  Libera nos, Domine!

A. D. GODLEY.

WILLIAM OF WYKEHAM, FOUNDER OF NEW COLLEGE
d. 1404
From a picture at New College (Oxf. Hist. Portr. Exhn., 1904, No. 2).

THE mediaeval student, like his modern successor, had many other things to do beside study. But this duty was not likely to be neglected in days when a poor man's only chance to rise was by his brains, and when learning could only be acquired from lectures. Hence the mediaeval course, mysterious as it appears to us, with its absence of examinations and with its constant logical disputations, meant a real intellectual discipline and brought the best men to the front; a single college, Merton, in the fourteenth century gave six archbishops to the see of Canterbury.

The course was summed up in the old lines:

Gram. loquitur, *Dia.* vera docet, *Rhet.* verba colorat;
Mus. canit, *Ar.* numerat, *Geo.* ponderat, *As.* colit astra;

which may be rendered thus into doggerel:

'Tis Grammar teaches how to speak,
   'Tis Logic sifts the false from true,
'Tis Rhetoric by which we deck
   Each word with its own proper hue.

Arithmetic of number treats,
   And Music rules the Church's praise;
Geometry the round earth metes,
   Astronomy the starry ways.

The *Trivium*—Grammar, Logic (' Dialectic '), and Rhetoric—had to do especially with the training of man's powers.

The *Quadrivium*—Music, Arithmetic, Geometry, and Astronomy—dealt with their application to practical uses.

Interlude

THE MASQUE OF MEDIAEVAL LEARNING

The stage shall represent a meadow near Oxenford. There entereth a Praelector, *who shall thus address the assembly.*

Praelector. GENTLES assembled here in Oxenford
To view our panoply of pageantry,
Now 'midst historic scenes of great events
Shall we unfold to you an Interlude,
A quaint morality in olden guise ?

[*Pauses a moment as for assent.*

Then as Praelector I must needs expound
That ye may profit by our picturing.
Here to your eye shall presently appear
Two students, typical of all the rest
Who in all ages have assembled here—
The one who with the truer finer sight
Shall, when anon they pass before his gaze,
Choose Learning and her worthy satellites;
The other who, allured by Pleasure's song
And Folly's garish finery, shall fail
To see him who doth follow after them,
And risking all on nothing doubly lose.
See where they come. Now is the Masque begun.

Here are perceived in the distance the two students, who soon come forward and approach the Praelector.

Vain Student. Sweete Maister, of your rightwysness,
If that ye be of this citye,

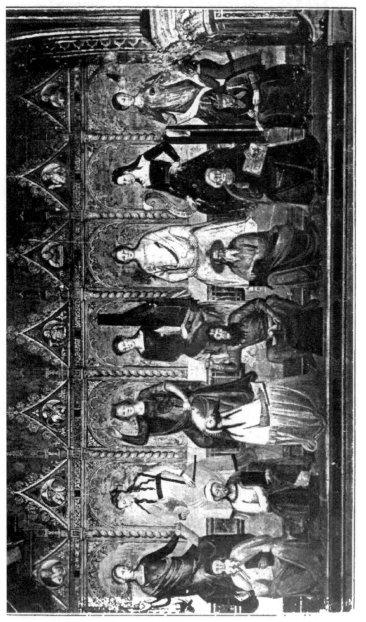

THE SEVEN LIBERAL ARTS

From the fresco in the Spanish Chapel in the Church of S. Maria Novella at Florence, of the School of Giotto, attributed by Ruskin to Simon Memmi. The order from right to left is (1) *Grammar*, showing the young aspirant the narrow gate, beneath is Priscian; (2) *Rhetoric*, and beneath, Cicero; (3) *Logic*, and beneath, Aristotle; (4) *Music*, with an organ, beneath, Tubal Cain; (5) *Astronomy*, lifting her right hand, beneath, Ptolemy; (6) *Geometry*, with a carpenter's square, beneath, Euclid; (7) *Arithmetic*, and beneath, Pythagoras. See Ruskin's *Mornings in Florence. V. The Strait Gate.*

          Instruct us in full gentleness
          How that it may ycleped be.
WISE STUDENT For we are of a far countrye,
          And seek a place hight Oxenford
          Where Learning is reputed lord.
PRAELECTOR. Then is your quest at length complete
          And ye may rest in full content;
          This is indeed the pleasant seat
          Where Learning holds her parlement
          So that all ears to her are bent.
          Would ye too join her business
          To profit you of her largess?
WISE STUDENT. Soothly for that we journeyed here;
          We pray you tell us, of your grace,
          How may one at her court appear?
PRAELECTOR. Why, even here; for in this place
          Her waiting ladyes seek their bower,
          While of some problem they descant
          Or raise clear-voiced some ancient chant.

Here shall a sound of singing be heard, and the PRAELECTOR shall in dumb show advise the students that it is even as he had said, and that the Court of Learning draw near.

Then there shall appear from the Right of the Assembly, DIVINITY, MEDICINE, and LAW, with their several trains. They sing:

Vide qui nosti literas,	Diligenter considera,
et bene doces vivere,	si sis actor, quid doceas,
quid sit doctrina litere,	et quod doces hoc teneas,
de quo et ad quid referas.	ne tua perdant opera
	aeternae vitae praemia.

VAIN STUDENT. Maister, I pray you in good sooth to tell
          Who be these Queens in glorious apparel?
PRAELECTOR. This Ladye who doth all exceed
          In lovely thought and gentle deed
          Is hight, I guess, Divinity,
          And teacheth immortality—
          How we shall live as best we may,

Fitting our duty to our day,
That having made a goodly end
We may to Paradise ascend.
Beside her Faith and Hope-the-Brave,
Who help her many souls to save.
Medicine, next Divinity,
Doth teach the cure of the body,
And maketh Melancholy be
Health's ward in cheerful chancery.
And after these in royal awe,
The consort of great monarchs, Law;
For she by dint of equity
Maketh men dwell in unity.
There Retribution walks behind,
With careful Justice, who is blind,
Yet doth Law's inmost secrets share
For that her counsel is so fair.
Choose then who doth you most joyance
And offer her allegiance.

Then shall the THREE SCIENCES *advance to their thrones. They sing:*

Vide, qui colis studium
pro Dei ministerio,
ne abutaris studio
suspirans a dispendio

lucri, nec te participem
coniunge vitae vitio,
namque multos invenio
qui sunt huius participes
ecclesiarum principes.

WISE STUDENT. Sir, I have chosen sweet Divinity,
If that I may her faithful liegeman be.

*Then he shall seek to approach her while the following is being sung, but as he
starteth so to do, shall the* SEVEN ARTS *coming forward bar his way.
They sing*

Vide, qui Dei munere
Dei colis gloriam
summi per Dei gratiam,
ne te possit decipere

neque trudat in vitium
Philisteus improvide,
clam te prodente Dalide,
ut non amittat meritum
Deus suorum militum.

WISE STUDENT. But, Maister, rede to me, I humbly pray,
    Why do these seven ladies bar my way?
PRAELECTOR. These be the Arts, who, ere you gain access
    Unto the Sciences their mistresses,
    Must each instruct you in her wisdom sage.
    First, Grammar, who doth govern verbiage,
    Logic, who doth the rule of Reason teach,
    And Rhetoric, with silver-sounding speech,
    Arithmetic, who numbers all the sands,
    And Music, with her cittern in her hands,
    Geometry, to whom the earth is given,
    And last, Astronomy, who scales the heaven.
    If still then to your purpose you adhere
    'Tis meet you should submit to their danger.
WISE STUDENT. Sir, I do beg you with humility
    You shall commend me to their curtesy

✿❦✿

THE BALADE OF FOOLISHE DESIRE

VAIN STUDENT. Such life is not for me, I guess,
    Nor is long service to my bent;
    Study to me is heaviness,
    And such was never mine intent.
    Too much for too small gain were spent
    If Pleasure ne'er would be my friend:
    If I should labour without end
    Of learning I should soon repent.

    Never to meet sweet Idleness,
    Nor to fair Folly give assent;
    Never to tourney with Noblesse,
    Nor ever know Amour's torment;
    To pore upon some document
    When thro' the casement. sang the Spring—
    This were indeed a grievous thing,
    And learning I should soon repent.

I speak, Sir, in all humbleness,
Yet have I heard such things anent,
That one may without wickedness
In other manner gain content.
Wisdom herself cannot prevent
The learned tribe from being fools
For all the teaching in her schools,
So that their learning they repent.

ENVOY

Therefore, Beau Sire, in gentleness,
Seeing that I will not assent
To Wisdom's dreary worthiness,
But would on Pleasure's path be sent,
Instruct me how that I may find
A mistress suited to my mind.

Then shall there suddenly appear in the distance the rout of FOLLY *and of*
PLEASURE, *who shall advance in procession thus singing:*

Meum est propositum   tunc cantabunt laetius
in taberna mori,   angelorum chori:
ubi vina proxima   'Deus sit propitius
morientis ori;   huic potatori.'

Here shall they pause for a moment.

VAIN STUDENT.   Ah! these are many times more fair,
More lovely, sweet and debonair.

They sing again:

Poculis accenditur   mihi sapit dulcius
animi lucerna;   vinum de taberna,
cor imbutum nectare   quam quod aqua miscuit
volat ad superna;   praesulis pincerna.

Here shall they pause opposite to the SCIENCES *and* ARTS.

PRAELECTOR.   This is the wicked rout of pleasurance
        That with fair seeming lureth' men to fall.
        Pleasure herself and Folly lead the dance,
        Offering cups with many a luring call,
        Whose wine sweet-tasting soon is turned to gall.
        And they that follow them must surely die:
        There is indeed no other remedy.

        Next cometh Pride-of-Life in glorious guise,
        And then in turn Gaming and Venery;
        Red War, who tempteth e'en the grave and wise,
        With Riches no less masterful than he;
        After whom cometh loutish Gluttony.
        And they that follow them must surely die:
        There is indeed no other remedy.

        Beau Sire, beware and mark well what you do!
        Next sluggish Sloth drags wearily along
        The Bishop Golias and his motley crew;
        And lastly Bacchus and his lustful throng,
        Mingling their ribald jests with drunken song.
        And they that follow them must surely die:
        There is indeed no other remedy.

Then shall the rout of FOLLY *pass in front of the* ARTS, *who shall sing*:

    Ieiunant et abstinent   et, ut opus faciant
    poetarum chori,   quod non possit mori,
    vitant rixas publicas   moriuntur studio
    et tumultus fori,   subditi labori.

During this the VAIN STUDENT *has been eagerly examining the procession with looks of great pleasure. The* PLEASURES *sing*:

    Unicuique proprium   me ieiunum vincere
    dat natura munus;   possit puer unus,
    ego nunquam potui   sitim et ieiunium
    scribere ieiunus,   odi tamquam funus.

During this shall they have paused, having passed by the throne of the SCIENCES, *and* FOLLY *and* PLEASURE *beckoning luringly to the* VAIN STUDENT; *he, hesitating for a little while, goeth to them. Twining him round w th garlands they do drag him out singing, and then may one perceive* TIME *following after them full silently. They sing :*

Feror ego veluti
sine nauta navis,
ut per vias aeris
vaga fertur avis,

non me tenent vincula,
non me tenet clavis,
quaero mihi similes,
et adiungor pravis.

When they have passed away, TIME *following, shall the* ARTS *and* SCIENCES, *particularly* DIVINITY, *since he hath chosen her his mistress, conduct the* WISE STUDENT *forth in the opposite direction preceded by the* PRAELECTOR, *who, when they are approaching the exit, shall let them pass him by, and then follows them out, and as they go they shall sing this .*

Iste mundus
furibundus
falsa praestat gaudia
quae defluunt
et decurrunt
velut campi lilia.

Res mundana
vita vana
vera tollit praemia,
nam impellit
et submergit
animas in Tartara.

Quod videmus
vel tacemus
in praesenti patria,
dimittemus

vel perdemus
quasi quercus folia.

Res carnalis
lex mortalis
valde transitoria,
frangit, transit
velut umbra,
quae non est corporea.

Conteramus,
confringamus
carnis desideria,
ut cum iustis
et electis
caelestia nos gaudia
gratulari
mereamur
per aeterna saecula.

Here endeth the Masque of Mediaeval Learning.

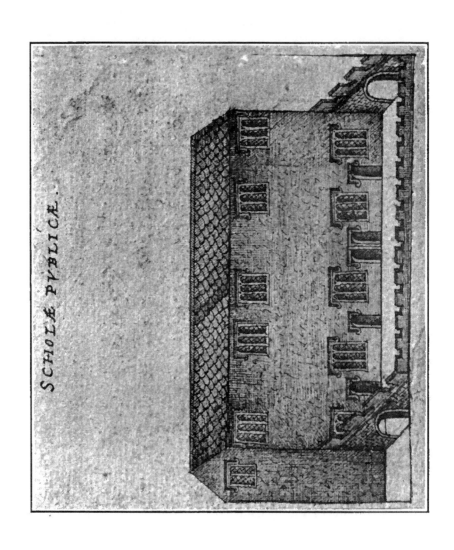

SCHOLÆ PVBLICÆ.

THE mediaeval course appeared narrow and barbarous to the men of the Renaissance, who were full of the new world of beauty and learning which was opened to them by the revived study of Greek. Such a man was Wolsey, himself 'a scholar and a ripe and good one'. Things looked bright for Oxford when Erasmus could write: 'When I listen to Colet, I seem to be listening to Plato himself. What has Nature formed softer or sweeter or pleasanter than the disposition of Thomas More?' It was for scholars like these that Wolsey built his magnificent College.

THE SOCIETY OF NEW COLLEGE IN 1463

The close of the Mediaeval period is well illustrated by this unique representation from a New College MS. of a complete College. The Warden, with Doctors of Theology, Medicine, and Law at his side, stand before the Masters of Arts; below are the junior Fellows and Choristers. In the background are the Hall, Chapel, and Cloisters of the College.

HENRY VIII AND WOLSEY

A.D. 1518

SCENE :—OXFORD. BEFORE THE MONASTERY OF ST. FRIDESWIDE.

Enter from L. a number of clerks conversing together. At the same time enter, from the centre, a scholar of Corpus, a pale, peaked, acid-looking individual with lank hair. He is apparently consumed with rage. In one hand he has tightly clenched a bundle of manuscript; with the other he clutches convulsively at his throat.

SCHOLAR. SPURNED !—slighted !—laughed at !—thrown into
   my teeth !
  Verse that Menander might have made.
    [*He turns and furiously shakes his fist towards
    the entrance.*
      Red fiend !
   The clerks come up behind him.

1ST CLERK. 'Tis Kitts of Corpus.
2ND CLERK.   What 's amiss ?
3RD CLERK.   What Gods
  Have made thee mad ?
1ST CLERK.   What fiend ?
SCHOLAR. [*fiercely facing them*]   The Cardinal !
    [*They shrink back alarmed. The* SCHOLAR *holds
    out his MSS.*
SCHOLAR. My verses are forbid. The King must hear
  No Greek. Another play 's preferred. Know ye
  With what trite tongue they will this day profane
  The royal ears ?
1ST CLERK.   With Latin ?
SCHOLAR.   No !

2ND CLERK.   French ?

SCHOLAR.   No !

3RD CLERK.   Not English ?

SCHOLAR.   English ! aye—the vulgar tongue—
The common speech wherein the unlettered hinds
Chaffer for farthings with the citizens.

> [*The clerks hold up their hands amazed.*

1ST CLERK.   And this is Oxford !

2ND CLERK.   Gods !

3RD CLERK.   *O tempora !*

SCHOLAR.   Words that Thalia whispered in my ear—

> [*Pathetically holding out his parchment MSS*

1ST CLERK.   We'll hear them.

2ND CLERK.   Yes, let's have them now.

SCHOLAR.   But—now ?

3RD CLERK.   Even now.

SCHOLAR.   Here ?

1ST CLERK.   Here.

SCHOLAR.   If you compel me—

2ND CLERK.   Read !

> [*He unrolls his MSS. and strikes an attitude.*
> *The others sprawl in semicircle round him*
> *on the grass. Two other clerks have entered*
> *and are passing behind the group.*

SCHOLAR. [*reads*] ᾿Ω Θεοί, βλέποιτ' ἂν οἷος ἐξ οἵων ἔφυν,
γναμπτὸς γὰρ ὢν τὸ σῶμα, Χριστοφόρου πατρός—

> [*As he finishes the line one of the two clerks*
> *springs at him, clouting him with a sound-*
> *ing whack on the back.*

3RD CLERK.   Thou filthy Greek !

> [*He knocks the* SCHOLAR's *hat over his eyes, trips*
> *him, and throws him on his face.*

4TH CLERK.   Thou monstrous wooden ass !
Thinkest thou to void thy Greek into our streets
While Ilium's sons look on ?

> *[The other clerks, recovering from their first*
> *stupefaction, scramble hastily to their feet.*

1ST CLERK.   Trojans forsooth!
2ND CLERK. Up, Greeks, and down them!
3RD CLERK.   Insolents!

> *[The two Trojans have taken to their heels.*
> *Four or five Greeks pursue them as far as*
> *the side, then give up the chase and return.*

1ST CLERK.   They run
Like Hector.
2ND CLERK.   And we lack our spears.

> *[A group of citizens, among whom are a butcher,*
> *a tailor, and the host of the Bull Inn, have*
> *entered and drawn near the Scholar of Corpus,*
> *who has picked himself up and stands*
> *smoothing his MSS.*

SCHOLAR.   What though,
History cannot lie. We Greeks *must* win.
1ST CLERK. By ZEUS we shall!
2ND CLERK.   Well said. Read on.
3RD CLERK.   Aye, read.

> *[They throw themselves down again.*

SCHOLAR. [*reads*] Ὦ Θεοί, βλέποιτ' ἂν οἶος ἐξ οἴων ἔφυν,
γναμπτὸς γὰρ ὢν τό—

> *[As he finishes the first line a burly butcher,*
> *who has come up behind, plucks him by the*
> *sleeve. He turns angrily.*

BUTCHER. Good master scholar, at what hour comes the King?
SCHOLAR. Never—if I know aught. (*venomously*)
BUTCHER.   How never—why?
SCHOLAR. The King's afeared.
BUTCHER.   Afeared!—of what?
SCHOLAR.   The pest—
The sweating sickness.

> *[A perceptible shudder passes through the crowd.*

TAILOR. [*crossing himself*]   Holy saints!

OLD WOMAN. [*softly*]   O God!

> [*She bends her head and, turning apart, stands
> sobbing silently.*

BUTCHER.   Thou liest, tallow-face, the King's no coward.

SCHOLAR.   I say the sweating sickness—

HOST.   Peace! name it not;
The word breeds malady.

OLD MAN. [*shrill-voiced*]   The name of death
Falls not so cold on the ear.   Prithee no more.

> [*He takes the* BUTCHER *by the arm, points to the*
> OLD WOMAN, *and says in lower tones*

Poor dame—last month—husband, and two stout sons.

> [*The group moves away.   The* BUTCHER, *as he
> passes the* OLD WOMAN, *lays his hand for a
> moment on her shoulder in silent sympathy.
> A couple of black-robed Benedictine monks
> cross the scene, going out at the centre.   More
> citizens come on.*

SCHOLAR.   Thou burly brute! [*looking after the* BUTCHER]

1ST CLERK. [*softly*]   The pest will pay your score;
So big a mark is not twice missed.   Read on.

SCHOLAR. [*reads*] Ὦ Θεοί, βλέποιτ' ἂν οἷος ἐξ οἵων ἔφυν,
γναμπτὸς γὰρ ὢν τὸ σῶμα, Χριστοφόρου πατρός—

> [*As he finishes the first line a horseman enters
> from the direction of Abingdon Road, shouting*

HORSEMAN.   The King, the King's at hand.   Bestir yourselves!

> [*At once all is movement.   The rider goes out
> through the centre entrance.   More citizens
> come on and more clerks.   'The King!
> the King!' is in every mouth.   The sprawl-
> ing clerks spring to their feet.   The butcher
> and tailor group move down towards the
> opposite corner of the scene.*

1ST CLERK. We'll hear it anon.
2ND CLERK. Another day.
SCHOLAR. [*piqued*] For me,
I had as lief not read.
BUTCHER. The King afeared!
Ho! ho! I knew he lied.
TAILOR. Nay, I have heard—
[*The* BUTCHER *takes him by the ear.*
BUTCHER. I've heard thy tongue clacks oftener than thy shears.
The devil will have thee for a gossip friend
An thou heed not. [*The* TAILOR *frees himself.*
TAILOR. Nay, friend, *thou* liest there!
BUTCHER. I lie!
TAILOR. I'll prove it so.
OLD MAN. What proof?
TAILOR. I'll prove
The devil ne'er can come by me.
BUTCHER. Go to!
OLD MAN. Come, prove it!
HOST. How?
[*The* TAILOR *mysteriously produces from an inner
pocket a very dirty piece of paper which
he unfolds before them.*
TAILOR. In this the Pope doth swear
That I shall go to heaven. Therefore, thou liest.
OLD MAN. 'Tis an indulgence?
TAILOR. Bought of a Pardoner,
A friar, for fivepence and a pot of ale.
OLD MAN. Heaven for fivepence!
BUTCHER. Canst thou read the words?
[*The* TAILOR *looks blankly at the paper a moment.*
TAILOR. I?—No; canst thou?
[*Giving it to the* BUTCHER, *who turns it over
twice.*
BUTCHER. No.
[*The* OLD MAN *takes it and peers into it.*

OLD MAN   No.

                           `[*Gives it to the* HOST.

HOST. [*indignantly*]   No! At 'The Bull'
     Fivepence would buy thee twenty quarts of ale;
     With that thou might'st have been in heaven now.
                 [*He throws the indulgence at the* TAILOR'*s head.*

The Cardinal's guard enter, in scarlet coats bordered with black velvet. After them gentlemen of his household, bareheaded, with their bonnets in their hands, in crimson velvet and gold chains Next two silver crosses borne before him, then four priests carrying silver pillars and poleaxes. - Next, on a scarlet cushion, is borne the Cardinal's hat; and lastly, the CARDINAL *himself in scarlet. His right hand is raised to bless the crowd, many of whom kneel. A fanfare of trumpets proclaims the arrival of the King's party. First come the heralds in their livery, then a band of royal archers in the Tudor livery of green and white with a large* 𝕳 *back and front. After them follow* HENRY *and* CATHERINE *of* ARAGON *on horseback, attended by* SIR THOMAS MORE, PACE, *the King's secretary, the physician* LINACRE, TUNSTALL, *the master of the robes, and a number of ladies and gentlemen, amongst whom are* SIR THOMAS BULLEN'*s* DAUGHTERS, MARY *and* ANNE. *The* KING'*s appearance is greeted with an outburst of wild cheering. Women wave their 'kerchiefs and men fling their caps in the air. The* KING *reins his horse, and immediately at a signal from* SIR THOMAS MORE *the procession halts. Grooms spring forward to the royal bridles.* WOLSEY *advances to greet the royal pair.*

HENRY. [*lustily*] Our dear Lord Cardinal! Stay, stay—
     We will descend—
                 [*He springs from his horse.* MORE *dismounts the*
                   QUEEN, WOLSEY *bends as though about to kneel.*

WOLSEY.   Sweet welcome to your Grace.
HENRY.   Rise, for you are the pillar of our State
     And may not bend.
                     [*He raises and embraces him.*

         You look not well in health;
  Take heed.

WOLSEY.   My health is in your service, sire;
In that I am ever well.

         [He kisses the QUEEN's *hand.*

       Madam, you bring
The sunshine in your train.

QUEEN.   My lord I bring
The sun. *[laying her hand on the* KING's *shoulder]*

WOLSEY.   'Tis true. I think this royal sun
Must sure o'erawe the elements and time,
And make this day in Oxford's story shine
To the end of memory. I pray you sit,
Whiles to your Majesties I may unfold
The purport of your coming.

      [He conducts them towards two chairs of state
      which have been placed in an oblique line
      somewhat to the right of the scene. As
      they advance towards them a very small
      boy in miniature academic robes is thrust
      forward from the crowd by a SCHOOLMASTER.

KING. *[halting]*   What is this?

WOLSEY. I know not.

SCHOOLMASTER. *[bowing]* May it please your Grace. Speak, Ned
             [to the boy.]

      [The infant's shrill treble immediately pipes
      out the following lines of Latin verse.

BOY.   Carmina nostra Iovis magni cere- comminuant -brum,
Volcani quali labefecit volnere plaga,
Pallas ut armata ex ore effundatur hiulco,
Omnia mortales omnes docuisse parata.

      [As he finishes the boy runs back and hides his
      face in the schoolmaster's gown. The KING
      roars with laughter.

KING.   Good lad, wast born with Latin in thy mouth?

QUEEN.   When hath he time for English? [*laughing.*]
SCHOOLMASTER [*proudly*]   God forbid,
   Your Grace, that son of mine should e'er be learned
   In English before Latin.

     [*During this incident the horses are led off, and
      the Courtiers cross unobtrusively behind the
      central group, and range themselves at the
      back of the royal chairs. HENRY hands
      CATHERINE to her seat.*

HENRY. [*sitting on her right*]   Now, my lord
WOLSEY. Your Grace—the purpose I would here unfold,
   Hath so entwined its roots about my soul,
   It scarce may be unravelled. Here, in brief,
   By the abbey church of holy Frideswide,
   Have I a college planned, that like a crown
   Shall grace the brows of Oxford, and unite
   All houses closer 'neath her sovereignty.
HENRY.   A good device. What of endowments—funds?
   For colleges, like men, live not on air
WOLSEY. Out of decay springs life.

     [*He takes a parchment from one of two secre-
      taries*

        Herein are named
   Some twenty priories, whose withered frames
   Cry for the mercy of the grave. I think
   To put these revenues to better use.

       [*He hands it to the KING.*

MORE.   Now does the builder start with pulling down!
        [*Aside to PACE.*

PACE.   God knows where that will end!
HENRY. [*frowning at the paper*]   Lord Cardinal,
   Who treads on holy ground needs pick his steps.
   Will the Pope suffer this?
WOLSEY.   His holiness,
   (I am advised from Rome) so cherishes

CHRIST CHURCH

From the Oxford Almanack of 1724, the realization of the dreams of the present episode.
The Cathedral, Tom Quad, the Hall, and Tower are well depicted, and the figure of Mercury
in the centre of the quadrangle should be noted. In front are King Henry VIII and Cardinal
Wolsey ('Ego et Rex meus').

The peace and safety of your Grace's realm,
That he will suffer it.

HENRY.   Good news, i' faith!
Those words have from our conscience plucked a thorn
Were like to have troubled it. But for our realm,
'Tis not on clerkship that its safety hangs.
We trust, my lord, to this [*laying his hand on sword*]
     sooner than all
Your colleges and clerks in Christendom.

                              [*He returns the parchment.*

WOLSEY. Your Grace must pardon me, for I am old;
A man well up the hill of life who tries·
To pierce the horizon of the impending years.
A change has come of late, I know not how,
Upon the means of men. Might is not all;
Shrewd thinking now wins further than stout blows.
The old arms rust, but from the new-forged steel
Come flashings bright with thought. I pray your Grace
Forget that here are colleges or clerks;
Only remember here be men who think,
And even as the brain is master to the hand,
The master of the nation's task is here.
Here let us build, but not with stones alone;
Let's build with courage, faith, and enterprise,
With daring and a challenge to the unknown,
And most with honesty. Let's build a house
Wherein by spirit-subtle alchemy
Men may transform the wise high thoughts of old
To new and golden deeds. Then shall we build
As I have dreamed we built. Majestic walls
Wherein the brain of England shall conceive
The thoughts that on white-winged ships shall fly
To wake the slumbering barriers of the world;
Sky-soaring towers whose every stone shall be
The mother of a city far away.
The scholar's taper in his room on high

Shall be a star to pierce the utmost dark,
And guide poor men. From hence shall justice flow,
And truth, to fill the healing founts of law;
Schemes shall be laid, imperial ventures born,
Young hands shall sow the seed of government,
Young hearts and noble minds shall make this place
An altar sacred with their sacrifice,
And over it 'The Lord my Light' shall shine
On England's destiny. This is my dream—
God send it to come true.

HENRY.   Amen!

WOLSEY. [*to* CATHERINE]   Your Grace,
A rascal Greekless and unlatined clerk
Hath writ an allegory to be played,
'Tis called 'The Coming Chivalry'.
Since beauty still should queen it in the lists
Your Grace shall throw your glove into the field
And we'll abide the issue.

CATHERINE. [*flinging her glove*]   So, my Lord.

Enter a YOUNG KNIGHT *on a hobby horse. His surcoat is all of white. On his breast he bears a silver sun. His shield is a sun argent on an azure field. He is armed with helm, sword and lance in rest. He picks up the* QUEEN's *glove, holding aloft.*

KNIGHT   'Tis a shrine where lingers
Scent of flower-like fingers,
The spirit of the royal fair
That lately did inhabit there.
By that spirit here I swear,
Swear upon this altar,
Ne'er to fail or falter
In faith or truth or homage to her favour that I wear.

                    [*He fastens the glove to his helm   Enter
                    a* FAIR SPIRIT *clad in green. She moves
                    with uplifted head and eyes fixed on the*

sky.   In one hand she bears a lighted
torch.   The KNIGHT *wheels round and*
faces her.

KNIGHT.   Art thou spirit, nymph, or dryad,
    Or a lost and wandering Pleiad?
    For like exiled stars thine eyes
    Pitifully yearn toward the skies.
SPIRIT.   The Spirit of the Age am I.
KNIGHT.   Wherefore dost bend thy looks on high;
    What seek'st thou?
SPIRIT   I seek truth;
    Who art thou?
KNIGHT.   I am youth.
    I seek adventure; tell me where
    I may find truth, for truth is fair.
SPIRIT.   I cannot.   'Tis not to be found,
    Not in the air nor on the ground,
    Nor anywhere that man may know.
KNIGHT.   Sore I must grieve if that be so.
SPIRIT.   Grieve not, Sir Youth, thy grief is fond;
    Truth was ordained to be beyond
    And yet be sought.
KNIGHT.   But if to nought
    The search come, not to seek were best
SPIRIT.   Not in the finding, in the quest
    The honour lies.
    Brave knights and wise
    Must seek till death shall bid them rest.
    Life is the chasing of the dream
    Of that which is, yet shall not be
    Till all the waters of the stream
    Have flowed into the sea.
KNIGHT.   Spirit, I pray,
    Point me the way;
    As I love honour let me die
    If I seek not truth eternally.

[The SPIRIT *waves her torch in the air.   Enter
a mimic castle with lofty gateway hung
with a tapestry.   It is borne by four men
within.   Before it dance a number of
nymphs, listening with hands to ears and
chanting to a buzzing, monotonous refrain.*

SONG.

Hear ye the bees!
In the flowers
'Neath the trees
They are busy,
And the hum,
Like a dizzy
Rolling drum,
How it quivers in the breeze;
Like the throbbing of the pulses, or the pattering of
    showers.
Hear ye the bees!

[The NYMPHS *bend forward, looking and pointing
at the ground.   The music becomes staccato.*

Watch ye the ants!
Through the grasses
O'er the plants
They are toiling,
And they run
Like the shining
Of the sun
Where its light at even slants
O'er the ruffling of the waters by the zephyr as it
    passes.
Watch ye the ants!

The castle stands in the centre of the scene.

SPIRIT.   Sir Youth, this house thy home must be :
          This is the Castle Industry.

In these high walls there is nought to hear
Of love-sick lutes, or the idle cheer
Of the song of sloth. There is nought to see
Of the poppied dreams of luxury.
Yet the life within is fair and free,
And ever and ever upon the air
Is the sound of a song so debonair
That the hearer's blood shall be caught and whirled
In tune with the 'great heart-beats of the world.

KNIGHT. Here let me dwell,
For it likes me well;
To north, to south, to east, to west,
From hence will I ride in the deathless quest.

SPIRIT. Youth, thou first must seek thy bride;
Maid and man go side by side.

KNIGHT. Then, Spirit, let me know where dwells
The fairest of fair damosels.

SPIRIT. The fairest damosel is she
Who hath this many a century
Been chained in dire captivity
By the power of the Dragon Ignorance.

KNIGHT. He shall die on the point of my good lance!

SPIRIT. Nor sword, nor helm, nor shield, nor lance
Avail with the Dragon Ignorance.
Cast them away!

KNIGHT. Spirit, I pray
How may I fight if my hands be bare?

SPIRIT. Enter! [*points to castle*] and bid them arm thee there.

The KNIGHT *rides into the castle.*

OLD MAN. How, think ye, will this Knight the Dragon slay?
BUTCHER. Give me a stout cudgel.
TAILOR.   Nay, I know:
He 's gone for one of yon new-fangled guns
To shoot the beast.
SCHOLAR.   Would he might use his gun

To shoot the poet beast that wrote this stuff.

> [*The crowd cries 'Hush!' The* Knight *re-*
> *appears. For helm he wears a scholar's cap,*
> *for surcoat a scholar's gown, for shield*
> *a book blazoned with the University's*
> *Arms, and in place of his lance an immense*
> *goose-quill, cut pen-wise, but innocent of ink.*

SPIRIT. Now, Heaven prosper thee, Sir Youth;
Well armed art thou for the quest of truth.

KNIGHT. Let me prove my arms in one brave bout;
Help me to seek this Dragon out.
I might take and bind him
In his lair.
Where shall I find him?

SPIRIT. Everywhere.
In camp, in court, in church, in state,
In cottage small, in castle great,
Where'er men be above the ground,
The Dragon Ignorance is found.

Enter the Dragon Ignorance, *humming hideously and breathing fire*
from his nostrils. Bound to him by a long fine gold chain,
attached to a golden girdle circling her waist, is a Maiden, *who*
moves with bent head and her face hidden in her hands.

SPIRIT. Lo, where he comes!

KNIGHT. The whole earth hums.
Hark to the hideous rumbling roar!

SPIRIT. 'Tis monkish Latin he's mumbling o'er.

KNIGHT. From either nostril, withering fires!

SPIRIT. The breath of bigots, the words of liars.

> [*The* Maiden, *raising her head, looks piteously at*
> *the* Knight.

KNIGHT. O fair as the face of heav'n! Her name?

SPIRIT. Knowledge, Sir Youth. Is thy soul aflame?

KNIGHT. An I free her not may I die of shame.

> [*He rides forward and confronts the* Dragon.

KNIGHT. Dark Dragon Ignorance, stand fast!
           For the hour hath struck that shall be thy last.

> [*He charges the* DRAGON, *plunging his plume*
> *deep into the* DRAGON'S *open jaws. With*
> *a roar, the beast rolls over, wriggles and*
> *dies ; when the* KNIGHT *withdraws his*
> *weapon the point is stained as black as ink.*
> *He flings the plume away, goes to the*
> MAIDEN, *and breaks her chain. As the*
> DRAGON *rolls over, the* KING, *whose tastes*
> *are spectacular, roars with laughter.*

BUTCHER. Why, there's a royal laugh—God bless him for't!
            As rich and juicy as a roast o' beef.

> [*The* KNIGHT *kneels before the* MAIDEN.

KNIGHT. Maid, in whose clear, far-visioned eyes
           The mirrored world I see,
           And the light of exalted destinies,
           Wilt thou be wife to me?

KNOWLEDGE. [*giving him her hand*]
             Sweet Knight, Sir Youth,
             We two shall go
             The way towards truth
             For evermoe.
             Take up thy lance.

> [*He picks up the quill and perceives the*
> *blackened point.*

KNIGHT. Unholy chance!
           What murky stain hath dimmed my weapon bright?

KNOWLEDGE. With that I'll teach thee deathless words to write.
             'Tis the Dragon's sable blood.
             Morning cometh out of night,
             Out of winter cometh spring,
             Out of darkness cometh light,
             Out of sleep awakening,
             And out of evil good.

[*The* Spirit of the Age, *who has moved up to the back of the scene, waves her torch aloft. The castle moves slowly towards the exit. Behind it the* Nymphs *dance back-wards, singing and beckoning* Youth *and* Knowledge, *who follow hand in hand.*

Nymphs. Hear ye the bees!
In the flowers
'Neath the trees
They are busy,
And the hum,
Like a dizzy
Rolling drum,
How it quivers in the breeze;
Like the throbbing of the pulses or the pattering of
showers.
Hear ye the bees!
[*As they disappear* Wolsey *steps forward.*

Wolsey. Now to St. Frideswide's.
[*He stops suddenly, seeing the* King *leaning back in his chair engaged in animated con-verse with a maid of honour. There is an awkward pause.*

Tailor. Thou seest yon maid?
'Tis Mistress Anne, Sir Thomas Bullen's girl.

Old Man. Eh, what? [*pressing forward to hear*]

Tailor. And I have *heard*— [*he whispers into the host's ear*]

Old Man. What, what, what, what?
[*The* Tailor *whispers to the* Old Man; *the* Host *whispers to the* Butcher.

Catherine. [*rising*] The play is done, your Majesty.

Henry. [*springing to his feet*] The play!
I' faith—and none too soon.
[*Then loudly, looking round with Royal bonhomie*
These Oxford clerks
Be merry mummers. We thank them heartily.

Lord Cardinal, let's on.

> [*A flourish of trumpets; the* CARDINAL *accompanies the* KING *and* QUEEN *out through the centre entrance. Their suites follow. As the* KING *and* QUEEN *disappear the* SCHOLAR *turns to his friends brandishing his MSS.*

SCHOLAR.   Now will ye hear
What these have lost?

1ST CLERK.   Yes!

2ND CLERK.   Read it!

3RD CLERK.   Read it now!

SCHOLAR. [*reads*]

'Ω Θεοί, βλέποιτ' ἂν οἷος—

4TH CLERK. A Greek, a Greek!

> [*Pointing him out to a crowd of other Clerks.*

ANOTHER.   Into the river!

ALL.   Aye!

> [*With a great shout they rush on the* SCHOLAR, *seize him and carry him out shoulder high, struggling, waving his MSS., and shouting out his verses.*

> *Exeunt omnes.*

JAMES B. FAGAN.

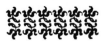

AS Mr. Lang writes, 'the intensely practical genius of the English race turned, not to letters, but to questions about the soul and its future, about property and its distribution.' The struggle of the Reformation began, and in it the University nearly perished. It was 'visited,' again and again, by Henry VIII's commissioners, by Edward VI's Protestant councillors, by Cardinal Pole under Mary. While men quarrelled about religion, the number of students fell away, the 'Schools' of the University were rented to washerwomen to dry clothes, and learning of all kinds decayed. It was just as Oxford was beginning to recover and hope for brighter days under Queen Elizabeth (1558–1603) that the tragedy of Amy Robsart occurred.

CUMNOR PLACE

AMY ROBSART

A. D. 1560

THE ninth episode represents a scene witnessed by the citizens of Oxford on Sunday, September 22, 1560. The tragedy of Amy Robsart's death is so familiar to readers of *Kenilworth* that a few words will suffice for introduction. Lord Robert Dudley, a son of Northumberland, the Protector, who governed England from 1549 to 1553, and a brother-in-law of Lady Jane Grey, had married, in 1550, the daughter and heiress of a Norfolk squire, Sir John Robsart. Immediately after the accession of Queen Elizabeth, in November, 1558, Lord Robert Dudley was known to be one of the Queen's favourites, and the affection she showed for him gave rise to some scandal. For three months in the spring of 1554, the Princess Elizabeth and Dudley had been fellow prisoners in the Tower of London, and their friendship probably dated from that period. In the summer of 1560, Amy Robsart, or, more properly, Lady Robert Dudley (she never was Countess of Leicester), was living at Cumnor Place, in the house of Anthony Foster, her husband's agent. On the evening of Sunday, September 8, her dead body was found at the foot of a staircase by some of the servants returning from Abingdon Fair. This is all that we know, and any suspicion that rests upon her husband depends solely upon the gossip that connected his name with the Queen's, and attributed to him the ambition of sharing the throne. The circumstances of his wife's death are not specially suspicious: she was not alone in the house at the time of its occurrence, and it may quite well have been an accident. The inquest threw no light upon the mystery. The episode represents the funeral procession to St. Mary's Church from Gloucester Hall (now Worcester College), whither the body had been brought from Cumnor. The procession, robed in black, passes by, chanting a solemn funeral dirge in the music of the period. The figure of Lord Robert Dudley himself is lacking, for, with a callousness which marked his whole conduct, he did not follow his wife to her grave in the chancel of St. Mary's. Her half-brother, whose name was Appleyard, was the chief mourner, and he was accompanied by Mrs. Norreys, the daughter of Lord Williams of Thame, a cousin of Amy Robsart's hostess at Cumnor. The scene represents Appleyard, bearing a great banner with the arms of Dudley and Robsart, walking at the foot of the coffin; Mrs. Norreys with her train-bearers; the Vice-Chancellor, Francis Babington, Master of Balliol, leading the procession with a large number of members of the University; two graduates with gowns, and wearing their hoods, in ancient fashion, on their heads, walk on each side of the coffin bearing each a small heraldic banner. The procession disappears in the distance on its way to St. Mary's, where the Master of Balliol, who preached the sermon, spoke of the poor lady 'so pitifully murdered'; and as it disappears the attention of the audience will be attracted by the sound of trumpets, heralding the approach of Queen Elizabeth, five years later. In that second procession, the figure of Robert Dudley, now Earl of Leicester, will no longer be looked for in vain.

ST. MARY'S CHURCH

THE mystery of the poor lady's death has never been cleared up, but men forgot all about it when the great Queen herself deigned to visit Oxford, and stayed for a whole week. She, like her subjects, had a perfect passion for pageants, but in these degenerate days we wonder how she could endure for three days in succession to listen to Latin disputations for four hours continuously in St. Mary's. The Queen did more for Oxford than 'visit' it; she 'did switch and spur on the industries' of the students by choosing the best of them for her service. Such an one was the ever famous Sir Thomas Bodley.

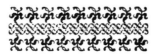

QUEEN ELIZABETH

From the Jesus College Picture (Oxf. Hist. Portr. Exhn., 1904, No. 85).

STATE PROGRESS
OF QUEEN ELIZABETH

A. D. 1566

SCARCELY have the last mournful notes of the funeral procession of Amy Robsart died away, when trumpet-calls may be heard beyond the bridge, growing more and more insistent. And now, on the other side of the water, the heads of the royal procession are seen to defile in slow state across the bridge. This is the gallant company, marshalled by Clarencieux of the Heralds, escorting the Queen on 'a marvelously serene Sunday' (Aug. 31, 1566) from Woodstock to enter her University and city of Oxford. The day before the Earl of Leicester, the Chancellor of the University, had visited the city to make the final arrangements for Her Majesty's reception, and on our left he is patiently waiting with the University procession to greet and welcome the Queen. The bells ring out in answer to the trumpets, and as the royal procession advances, the deputation from the University of Oxford, headed by their Chancellor, moves forward to meet it. (The actual place of meeting was at Wolvercote, two miles from Oxford on the Woodstock road.) With Leicester are the three Esquire Bedells carrying their staves, four Heads of Houses, including the Vice-Chancellor, who are Doctors, in their scarlet habits, and eight other Heads of Houses who are Masters of Arts. The Queen, it will be noted, is most sumptuously attired, and is borne in an open litter, and has in attendance on her the Spanish Ambassador, one marquis, five earls, two bishops, the Lord Chamberlain, and eight other peers, as well as her great Secretary of State, Sir William Cecil (Chancellor of the sister University of Cambridge), her ladies-in-waiting, her Yeomen of the Guard and Household Guard. Leicester and the Heads of Colleges are graciously permitted to kiss the Queen's hand, and an address of welcome in Latin is offered by a chosen orator; and now, headed by the University officials and Heads of Colleges, the royal procession moves on, where Mr. Mayor and his brother Aldermen, 'all in scarlet gowns,' accompanied also by a body of citizens, welcome Her Majesty to the city of Oxford. The Mayor delivers up his mace, which is handed back to him, and after an 'oration in English' and the gift of a 'silver-guilt' cup, the state procession once more winds along the road until the North gate of the city, called Bocardo (where St Michael's Church stands to-day), is reached. The street from here to Christ Church is lined by members of the University according to their degrees, who 'exhibit to the Queen an oration in writing and then certain verses' in order, Scholars first, then Bachelors, Masters, and Doctors, clad 'each in his habit and hood', and with loud cries of 'Vivat Regina Elizabetha!' taken up by the enthusiastic crowd. In the windows and on the roofs of the houses had also, we are told, collected 'the women and girls thinking to see' the sight; and so gradually Carfax—the place of Four Ways—at the top of the High Street is reached, where the Queen is greeted by the Professor of Greek in a Greek speech, to which Her Majesty deigns to reply briefly in the same tongue, to the joy of citizen and scholar alike. Amidst fresh acclamations and shouts of 'Vivat Regina!' drowning the trumpets and the bells, the Queen, 'passing still through the Scholars,' comes to the door of the Hall at Christ Church, where yet another oration is made. And here she descends, and with a canopy over her head, carried by four senior Doctors, she enters the Cathedral for service, at which, besides the sermon, 'the quyer sang and play'd with cornetes, *Te Deum.*' And this ends her formal entry; but a week was actually spent by Elizabeth in Oxford in various festivities, grave and gay, in academic disputations and a play, in reading and reciting of poems on the virgin sovereign; our last glimpse of her to-day, however, must be as she passes into the Cathedral through the kneeling and surpliced Scholars, and with the acclamation of 'Vivat Regina Elizabetha'' still ringing out from the loyal University and city.

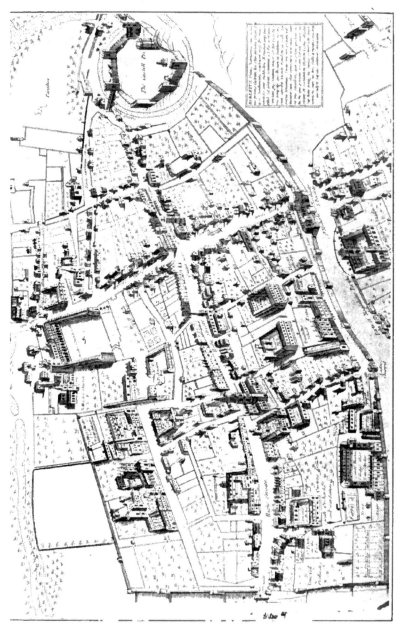

OXFORD IN 1578

The central part of Agas's celebrated bird's-eye view of Oxford, of which the only copy is in the Bodleian. It shows exactly what Queen Elizabeth saw in her royal visit to the city: the large amount of field and garden within the walls is noticeable.

IT was to a much more prosperous University that King James came in 1605. The King was proud of his learning, and when he saw the Bodleian, expressed the wish that he might end his days there, a captive chained like the books. He showed his appreciation by sending copies of his own books, which the courtly librarian welcomed in ' a pretty speech ', in which he said that probably Bodley himself had Paradise made happier for him by the glory of that day.

MERTON COLLEGE, FROM THE CHERWELL

JAMES I

A. D. 1605

Sir T. Bodley *and* Francis Bacon, *meeting.*

BODLEY.   WELCOME, welcome to Oxford, Mr. Solicitor-
General

BACON.   And welcome the occasion that brings me hither.
Truly, Sir, you may say, as one said of old, 'Funes
ceciderunt mihi in praeclaris.' As I journeyed, the
riverside meadows were full of the goodly scent of hay;
a pleasant exchange indeed for the foul air of the courts
of law, and the 'fumum et opes strepitumque Romae.'

BODLEY.   We of Magdalen College, Sir, deem we have the fairest
site in Oxford.

BACON.   And your meadows, I hear, are in springtime full of
fritillaries, or snake-heads, as the vulgar term them. A
rare flower, and passing delicate. I would fain beg, buy,
or borrow some for my garden at Gorhambury.

BODLEY.   They are wayward things, Sir, and strike their roots
deep. They will not grow in every soil. But, perchance,
your art and skill may, like grace, triumph over Nature.

BACON.   We can but conquer Nature by obeying her. But
enough of these toys. Is His Majesty yet arrived?

BODLEY.   He will be here anon. He has been heard of at Woodstock; and our revels are already toward. We poor
scholars cannot hold a candle to your town wits; but we
have one or two drolleries in preparation that may serve
His Majesty to yawn at, and pass away the time betwixt
dinner and supper; and Master Shakespeare and Heminge,

his fellow, have come down to Oxford, and are even now at the 'Crown'.

BACON.   What, for the Scotch play?

BODLEY.   Aye, Mr Solicitor, we are all Scotchmen now. Nothing goes down but what is from the further side of the Tweed. The baron of beef and my lady plum-pudding have had to make way for haggis and cockie-leekie.

BACON.   And beggarly Scots Knights, with long faces and long pedigrees, carry off our rich heiresses, like the Sabine women of old!

BODLEY.   Yet, methinks I remember, Sir, that a noted orator, our modern Marcus Tullius, delivered himself of late of a weighty speech in their favour.[1]

BACON.   You have me there, Sir. But, a word in your ear. We must not forget what the Spaniard says: 'As the prior sings, so must the sacristan respond.' I am but the poor sacristan. But to our play. I hold it but a one-sided piece. The best therein but tolerable, the worst is vulgar, foolish, and childish, unfit for the ears of Majesty.

BODLEY.   I have bidden Master Shakespeare to be in attendance, Sir, and I hear his voice, even now, at the gate.

Enter SHAKESPEARE.

Give ye good day, Master Shakespeare.

SHAKES.   Good-day to you, gentlemen both.

BODLEY.   Be covered, Master Shakespeare, and, prithee, be seated on this joint-stool.

BACON.   We would fain have some discourse with you, touching that part of your—your—Scotch play—Macpherson—Mac—beshrew me, but I forget the name.

SHAKES.   [*tentatively*] Macbeth?

BACON.   Aye, aye, Macbeth, so indeed it was.

BODLEY.   The play, I understand, was well liked in London.

SHAKES.   It had, Sir Thomas, as good success as it deserved.

BACON.   Master Shakespeare, you speak in riddles, like an oracle.

[1] Speech on Naturalization of the Scots, 1607.

ST. GILES'S, AND ST. JOHN'S COLLEGE

This broad thoroughfare, extending from the Martyrs' Memorial to St. Giles's Church, was well adapted for a royal entrance to Oxford. The stage on which the Witches' scene was acted in 1605 was just by the stone gateway which may be noticed beneath the tree at the edge of the enclosure which still secludes St. John's from the public road.

SHAKES.   [*smiling*] And truly, Mr. Solicitor, if I do, I am inspired
by the genius of the place.

BACON.   That is it, Sir; that is what I fain would say—the genius
of the place, and the genius of the time. Methinks,
Master Shakespeare, and in submission to your better
judgement [*takes MS from* SHAKESPEARE], such lines as
these [*reads contemptuously*]
    'Eye of newt and toe of frog, &c.'
savour more of Canidia and her vile crew than is fitting
in a royal presence. [*Reads*]
    ' Nose of Turk and Tartar's lips, &c.'

SHAKES   In sooth, Master Solicitor, the lines are more fit for the
ears of the groundlings than for those of his sacred
majesty. We of the stage have this necessity laid upon
us by our art; we take, like the chameleon, the colour of
what is about us; we cannot be what we would be, but
what others would have us be.

BACON.   Even so, but here you have a princely audience, before
whom it would ill beseem you to utter things unworthy
of your hearers. . . . Then you are willing for the time
being to leave out those lines?

SHAKES.   At your pleasure, Mr. Solicitor.

BODLEY.   This will stand [*reads*]. ' How now, ye secret black
and midnight hags,' and so forth; and the apparitions, as
they are set down.

SHAKES.   With your leave, gentlemen both, I would make some
few changes at the end. My fellow, John Heminge, and
I have devised some antastic conceits, which we would
fain keep secret till the scene be acted. We have brought
our own players down from London, and we trust our
poor endeavours may not fall short of expectation.

BACON.   So be it then, Master Shakespeare. But I would have
you bear in mind that His Majesty, Heaven bless him,
is a scholar, and hath the tongues, as few princes have,
and that the audience, in their degrees, are all scholars,
and many ripe ones [*bowing to* BODLEY]. Were it not

too late, I would have you frame your lines after the manner of Terence, had he written in English. An you took him for your model, you could not do amiss.

BODLEY.   Well said, well said, Mr. Solicitor.

SHAKES   Methinks, gentlemen, had Terence been bred in Scotland, he would have been but a ballad-monger, and fed on oatmeal.

BODLEY.   And we should have had no Heautontimoroumenos.

SHAKES.   I crave your pardon, Sir, but such jaw-splitting words are past my comprehension.

BACON.   Ha! Ha! I trust, Master Shakespeare, you may never suffer from that distemper—you, I am sure, are no 'self-tormentor'. And so we take our leave of you.

SHAKES.   My service to you, gentlemen.

[BACON *and* BODLEY *retire apart and converse.*

Enter JOHN HEMINGE.

O goodman Jack, would thou hadst been here ten minutes ere this!

HEMINGE.   Why, why, what now? What has befallen, wherein have they angered thee?

SHAKES   Angered! nay; not angered; but, O Jack, though I could weep, yet I could die of laughing. Hast ever heard tell of Solomon?

HEMINGE.   Aye, aye, and seen him too wrought in the arras. But what of that? The King, they say, that now is, is the British Solomon.

SHAKES   Well, he may be. And I am the woful mother. Look not on me thus, Jack. I tell thee, I am the mother; and my bantling is to be cut in pieces before mine eyes. The weird sisters' song! they will have none of it.

HEMINGE.   Marry, the more fools they. Why, at the Blackfriars, 'twas applauded to the echo. I can hear the stamping and the hand-clapping even now.

SIR THOMAS BODLEY, FOUNDER OF THE BODLEIAN LIBRARY

SHAKES.   O Jack, if thou couldst have been here! [*Mimics* BACON's *manner of reciting 'Eye of newt,' &c.*] Believe me, I thought I should have had to feign nose-bleeding that I might hide my face. They would fain have the play [*chuckles*] like Terence! Faith, I must put myself to school again, and truly there is much need.

HEMINGE.   Then I could promise thee a taste of the birch.

SHAKES.   Enough, Jack, enough of that, while memory holds her seat in this distracted globe

                      [*Puts his hands to his head.*

HEMINGE   Be of good cheer, Will, we know what we know. We have that within our bosom and in our wardrobes which will give them whereof to make a nine days' wonder. Meanwhile, let's to the 'Crown' and crush a cup of sack.

SHAKES.   Have with you then! I have had enough to make a stockfish swear, and an anchorite thirsty, and the day is warm.

Enter JAMES I, *with procession of Court, on horse*

KING.   Upon my saul, a rare and goodly piece of work. [*Looking at Theatre*] The chiels in Lunnon couldna hae dune it better.

BACON.   Is it your Majesty's pleasure to admit to your royal presence, Sir Thomas Bodley, whom my poor wit cannot duly praise in words?

KING   Welcome, welcome, Sir Thomas Godly.

BACON.   [*murmurs audibly*] 'O felix culpa!'

BODLEY.   Your Majesty does me too much honour.

KING.   Nay, nay, Sir Thomas. For learning and godliness should aye be sib thegither.} It was Porcius Festus said to Paul, 'Thy much learning hath made thee mad,' but we Christian rulers are of another mind.

BACON.   In sooth your Majesty may well say so, being yourself a living and breathing library of all knowledge human

G

and divine wherein the mind of man can occupy itself.
Augustus had his Palatine;—but we . . .

KING.   Hout, mon, we best ken our ain frailty. We are
mortal, but this modern Palatine [*turning to* BODLEY] shall
last to benefit all posterity.

BODLEY.   In this roll your Majesty will find depicted the ground
plan of our new edifice [*gives it to the* KING, *who handles
it awkwardly and lets it drop*]. Permit me, Sir. Here
is Duke Humphrey's Library, now standing, which forms
one side of a quadrangle which I propose to build   It
will all be paved with stone.

BACON.   Nay, Sir, by your favour, I like not that. Stone
strikes cold to the feet, and holds the damp.

KING.   Aweel, aweel, settle it as ye will   We thank you,
Sir Thomas.   Why what have we here ?

[*Curtain rises, play begins.*

MACBETH (Act IV, Sc. 1)

[*Lines* 1–47; *then :*]

Enter MACBETH.

MACB.   How now, you secret, black, and midnight hags !
What is 't you do ?

ALL.   A deed without a name.

MACB.   I conjure you, by that which you profess,—
Howe'er you come to know it,—answer me :
Though you untie the winds and let them fight
Against the churches; though the yesty waves
Confound and swallow navigation up;
Though bladed corn be lodg'd and trees blown down;
Though castles topple on their warders' heads;
Though palaces and pyramids do slope
Their heads to their foundations; though the treasure
Of Nature's germens tumble all together,
Even till destruction sicken; answer me
To what I ask you.

FIRST WITCH.   Speak.

SEC. WITCH.   Demand.

THIRD WITCH.   We'll answer.

FIRST WITCH. Say if thou'dst rather hear it from our mouths,
    Or from our masters'?
MACB.   Call 'em: let me see 'em.
FIRST WITCH. Pour in sow's blood, that hath eaten
    Her nine farrow; grease, that's sweaten
    From the murderer's gibbet, throw
    Into the flame.
ALL.   Come, high or low;
    Thyself and office deftly show.

      Thunder. FIRST APPARITION *of an armed Head.*

MACB.   Tell me, thou unknown power,—
FIRST WITCH.   He knows thy thought:
    Hear his speech, but say thou nought.
FIRST APP. Macbeth! Macbeth! Macbeth! beware Macduff;
    Beware the Thane of Fife. Dismiss me. Enough.
                       [*Descends.*

MACB.   Whate'er thou art, for thy good caution thanks,
    Thou hast harp'd my fear aright. But one word more,—
FIRST WITCH. He will not be commanded: here's another,
    More potent than the first.

      Thunder. SECOND APPARITION, *a bloody Child.*

SEC. APP. Macbeth! Macbeth! Macbeth!—
MACB.   Had I three ears, I'd hear thee.
SEC. APP. Be bloody, bold, and resolute; laugh to scorn
    The power of man, for none of woman born
    Shall harm Macbeth.   [*Descends.*
MACB.   Then live, Macduff: what need I fear of thee?
    But yet I'll make assurance double sure,
    And take a bond of fate: thou shalt not live;
    That I may tell pale-hearted fear it lies,
    And sleep in spite of thunder.

Thunder. THIRD APPARITION, *a Child crowned, with a tree in his hand.*

                         What is this,
    That rises like the issue of a king,
    And wears upon his baby brow the round
    And top of sovereignty?
ALL.   Listen, but speak not to 't.

THIRD APP. Be lion-mettled, proud, and take no care
Who chafes, who frets, or where conspirers are:
Macbeth shall never vanquish'd be until
Great Birnam wood to high Dunsinane hill
Shall come against him.   [*Descends.*

MACB.   That will never be:
Who can impress the forest, bid the tree
Unfix his earth-bound root? Sweet bodements! good!
Rebellion's head, rise never till the wood
Of Birnam rise, and our high-plac'd Macbeth
Shall live the lease of nature, pay his breath
To time and mortal custom. Yet my heart
Throbs to know one thing · tell me—if your art
Can tell so much,—shall Banquo's issue ever
Reign in this kingdom?

ALL.   Seek to know no more.

MACB. I will be satisfied: deny me this,
And an eternal curse fall on you! Let me know.
Why sinks that cauldron? and what noise is this?
                                   [*Hautboys.*

FIRST WITCH. Show!
SEC. WITCH. Show!
THIRD WITCH. Show!
ALL.   Show his eyes, and grieve his heart;
Come like shadows, so depart.

A show of Eight Kings, the last with a glass in his hand: BANQUO's
Ghost following.

MACB.   Thou art too like the spirit of Banquo; down!
Thy crown does sear mine eyeballs: and thy hair,
Thou other gold-bound brow, is like the first:
A third is like the former. Filthy hags!
Why do you show me this? A fourth! Start, eyes!
What! will the line stretch out to the crack of doom?
Another yet? A seventh! I'll see no more:
And yet the eighth appears, who bears a glass
Which shows me many more; and some I see
That two-fold balls and treble sceptres carry.

*At this point the Stage is darkened, slow dirge-like music is played,
and the figure of* CHARLES I, *in Vandyck dress, but with the
face almost invisible, glides past, waving his hands as if in
farewell.*

KING.   This is baith strange and terrible.   I feel like to swoon.
How awful his action is, and why points he to his throat?
On my saul, I canna thole it mair.

BODLEY.   Stay, stay, your Majesty; it is over now: see, the sky
clears, and hark to the merry music.

The figure of CHARLES II *appears, richly dressed, and playing with
one or two spaniels; some light French dance is played, and
'When the King enjoys his own again.'*

KING.   An ugly black-a-vised carle! His face likes me not;
and his hair is as the hair of Absalom.   Pray Heaven
he escape from the oak-tree!   But this one hath misfortune
written on his very countenance.

Figure of JAMES II, *wrapped in a cloak, and carrying the Great Seal,
which he flings hastily away.*

KING.   Why, why,—what is that?
BACON.   [*in horror*] The Great Seal of England!
BODLEY.   Flung away like a thing of no account! What would
the Lord Chancellor, that now is, say to that, Mr. Solicitor-
General?
BACON.   Such things are no matter for jesting.

Figures of WILLIAM *and* MARY.

KING.   What, two together! I like not that.
BACON.   A Queen in her own right, methinks.
KING.   Marry, Mr. Solicitor, had her late Majesty taken to
herself a consort we perhaps had never crossed the Tweed.
BODLEY.   Therein she showed her wisdom, and we all have
cause to rejoice.   But who is this sorrowful creature?

Figure of QUEEN ANNE, *with her arm round the young* DUKE OF GLOUCESTER.

BACON.   The young Marcellus—and the weeping Octavia!
                    'Ostendent terris hunc tantum fata, neque ultra
                    Esse sinent.'

JAMES *rises hurriedly and bursts into tears.*

KING.   Forbear, forbear: this touches us to the quick. We too
                    know what it is to lose a bairn! My lords and gentle-
                    men, the hour is late—we have travelled far—and I—
                    I thank you, and farewell!

The Procession passes on.

ELIZABETH WORDSWORTH.

CHRIST CHURCH CATHEDRAL.

CHARLES I was as fond of Oxford as his father, and the University flourished greatly under him. At the height of his power, when he seemed likely to win in his struggle with the Parliament, he came down to see the new buildings which the ever generous Archbishop Laud had built for his own college. The garden front of St. John's, 'perhaps the most lovely thing in Oxford' (A. Lang), marks the climax of the happy days of the King.

PLATE XXVII

KING CHARLES I

From a picture by Edw. Bower, now at All Souls.
(Oxf. Hist. Portr. Exhn., 1905, No. 77.)

THE HAPPY DAYS OF
CHARLES I

A.D. 1636

THE name of King Charles I is more closely associated with Oxford than that of any other English sovereign, and the episode which commemorates this association is divided into three portions. In the summer of 1636, the King and Queen, with the Prince of Wales and the Duke of York, visited Oxford, and the Chancellor of the University, Archbishop Laud, was present in person to receive them. The scene represents the arrival of the royal barge, and its reception in the presence of a large crowd of citizens. After the formal reception of the sovereign, the royal party witness a pavane, an elaborate and stately dance which had been a favourite English dance since the reign of Henry VIII. The royal barge then moves slowly out of sight.

WHEN the King next came to Oxford, it was to turn it into
a camp and a court. For nearly four years Oxford was the
Royalist capital of England; its buildings became magazines for the
royal stores, and its students laid down their pens, and took up
the sword and the musket for 'Church and King'. 'The town
was full of lords and of persons of the best quality, with very many
ladies, who when not pleased themselves, kept others from being so,
as Clarendon quaintly (but no doubt truly) records.

PLATE XXVII

ARCHBISHOP LAUD
d. 1645
From a picture in the Bodleian.

PLATE XXIX

PRINCE RUPERT
From a picture by J. M. Wright at Magdalen.
(Oxf. Hist. Portr. Exhn., 1905, No. 142.)

THE EARLY DAYS OF THE CIVIL WAR

A.D. 1643

THE second portion of the episode represents the scene on July 14, 1643, when the Queen, who had been attempting to obtain assistance for her husband, entered Oxford in triumph. She had gallantly made her way southwards from the Yorkshire coast, in spite of attempts by the Parliamentary army to impede her progress. On July 11 Prince Rupert had met her at Stratford-on-Avon, and history tells that she was entertained by a granddaughter of William Shakespeare. Two days later, Charles himself met the Queen on the site of the battle at Edgehill in the preceding year, and on the 14th they reached Oxford. The scene represents the King as having gone on before his wife in order to give her a reception of greater ceremony. Accompanied by his body-guard, he rides out of the city to meet the State coach which conveys the Queen. The news of the Royalists' victory at Roundway Down on July 13 reaches Oxford at the moment of their meeting, and the King and Queen return to the city, with their escorts, amid the jubilant rejoicings of the crowd.

BUT all the loyalty of Oxford was vain. She had made herself an impregnable fortress, but the King at last sent orders for surrender. On June 24, 1646, Sir Thomas Fairfax entered, and took great pains the University buildings should not suffer from any Puritan iconoclasm. ' 'Tis said there was more harm done by the Cavaliers (during their garrison) by way of embezzilling and cutting off chains than there was since' is Wood's testimony respecting the treatment of the Bodleian.

THE EAST GATE

PLATE XXXI

MAGDALEN BRIDGE

View of Magdalen Tower and Bridge at the time of the Civil War. The original is in Magdalen College,
and was engraved by Skelton.

THE SURRENDER OF OXFORD

A.D. 1646

THE last portion of the episode is almost the last scene in the Civil War. In the spring of 1646, Charles's fortunes became desperate, and in the early morning of April 27 the King had escaped from Oxford in disguise. On May Day the Parliamentary forces began siege operations. The Governor, Sir Thomas Glemham, was anxious to fight to the last, but the King instructed him to surrender the town. Honourable terms were granted by Fairfax, and on a wet Midsummer Day, Wednesday, June 24, Glemham marched over Magdalen Bridge and through St. Clement's, at the head of the garrison, with colours flying and drums beating. The Roundhead troops lined the way on each side. The scene represents the march of the Royalist troops, while the victorious Roundheads chant one of the metrical versions of the 68th Psalm, a chant of victory which they employed on many occasions.

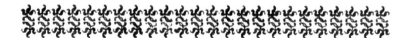

THE loyal students little expected that when next they saw soldiers in Oxford, they would be sent by the King to expel men whose only crime was that they had refused to break their statutes at royal command. But James II respected no man's conscience but his own. Nothing contributed more to break up the Cavalier alliance of 'Church and King' than the expulsion of the Fellows of Magdalen.

BIRD'S-EYE VIEW OF MAGDALEN

THE EXPULSION OF THE FELLOWS OF MAGDALEN

A.D. 1687

Enter the FELLOWS OF MAGDALEN, *headed by* DR. PUDSEY, DR. FAIRFAX, *and* DR. THOMAS SMITH. *Enter to meet them* PRESIDENT HOUGH.

DR. HOUGH. GENTLEMEN, being, as I am, the Head——
      DR. PUDSEY. Aye, our Head, well and truly elected!

FELLOWS. Aye! Aye!

DR. HOUGH. [*raising his hand*] Nay, I meant not that! I meant but to say that I am the Head and Front of your offence for which you must answer presently before the dreadful face of Majesty! And my mind misgives me, lest for my own gain or any stubbornness in fancied right I bring upon our House and you great woe. The wrath of Kings is very terrible.

DR. FAIRFAX. Yet is there a thing more terrible? For any fear of man——

DR. SMITH. Hush! You must not call His Sacred Majesty a man!

DR. FAIRFAX. To be false to religion and conscience! Is it not in our Statutes, clear as yonder sun, that he whom we elect for President must be of our House, or else of New College?

FELLOWS. Aye! Aye!

DR. FAIRFAX. And such a man have we elected! [*indicating* HOUGH] obeying every rule——

H

DR. SMITH. Except the King's will.

DR. FAIRFAX. Aye, Roguery, are you there?

DR SMITH. But answer me. If the King's will be law—

DR. FAIRFAX. I do answer you. If the King's will be law, and
that alone, and all our Statutes void, and void our oaths,
and we dispensed, and if Christ Church be rightly
Roman, and WALKER the Papist be lawful Master of
University—why then—why then—

DR. SMITH. [*triumphantly*] Aye, what then?

DR. FAIRFAX. Why, then, we are not Englishmen, nor Church
of England men, nor honest men, nor true men, nor
free men, but slaves and lickspittles!

DR. SMITH. [*raising his hands in horror*] Have a care!

DR. PUDSEY. The medicine is salutary, if bitter. [*He looks round.*]
We are agreed. We have a President, and, with submission to his sacred Majesty, and without thought of
resistance, a crime our souls abhor, we can elect no
other.

FELLOWS. Agreed! agreed!

Enter (L.), *with insolent airs,* OBADIAH WALKER, *Master of University,
followed at a little distance by the* DEAN OF CHRIST CHURCH,
BISHOP PARKER, CHARNOCK, *two or three* ROMAN PRIESTS, *and
a few of the populace.*

POPULACE. [*derisively singing*] Old Obadiah, sings Ave Maria!

CHARNOCK. [*turning one way*] Silence!

POPULACE. [*other side of him*] Old Obadiah, sings Ave Maria!

CHARNOCK. [*turning that way*] Silence!

DR. FAIRFAX. So will he soon silence us—the Popish hound!

DR. SMITH. [*clapping his hand on his mouth*] Do you think that
you reflect on the King's Majesty?

CHARNOCK. [*approaching the group of* FELLOWS] You must be gone,
Sir. [*To* HOUGH] The King wants not your presence.
Nor [*addressing* FAIRFAX] yours!

DR. FAIRFAX. Have you authority?

CHARNOCK. To bid you go? Yes!

HOUGH *and* FAIRFAX *retire* (*R*.) *dispirited; while the Popish group laugh and jest. Trumpets sound, bells break into melody, the City Companies march in and fill the background; then, preceded by* TROOPERS, *&c., enter the* KING, *followed by* JEFFREYS, *with the Great Seal borne behind him,* SUNDERLAND *with the Secretary's Seals, the* VICE-CHANCELLOR, FATHER PETRE, PENN *the Quaker,* LORDS, GENTLEMEN, *and* PAGES. *A* CHILD *with the scrofula is brought forward and touched: women in white strew flowers. The Roman group are graciously received and kiss hands. Then the* FELLOWS *are bidden forward and harshly addressed.*

THE KING. Did you receive my letter?

DR. PUDSEY. May it please your Majesty, we did.

THE KING. Then you have done very undutifully [*they fall on their knees and* PUDSEY *presents petition, which* KING *waves aside*]. You have been a stubborn, turbulent College in not electing him whom I commended to you! Is this your Church of England loyalty? Get you gone! Elect the Bishop of Oxford for your Head, Principal, what do you call it—

JEFFREYS. President, Sir.

THE KING. Aye, President of the College, or you must expect to feel the weight of my hand. [PUDSEY *offers petition again, which* JAMES *dashes to the ground*] Rise, and get you gone yonder, and instantly elect me the Bishop of Oxford, or you shall feel the weight of your Sovereign's displeasure.

> [*The* FELLOWS *retire sorrowfully to their former position, while the* KING *laughs and jests with the Roman group.*

THE KING. [*addressing the* LORDS COMMISSIONERS]. Do you stay, my lords, and receive their submission.

BP. OF CHESTER. And, may it please your Majesty, if they submit not?

THE KING. Do that you have in charge and fail not in your obedience. Gentlemen [*turning to Roman group*], I will satisfy you—or I will make empty seats enough!

VOICE. [*to the horror of circle*] Old Obadiah, sings Ave Ma—

THE KING. What was that?

BP. OF OXFORD. They cry, Sir, Ave imperator!

THE KING. 'Tis well.

> [*The* KING *withdraws* (R.) *amid bells and cannon, followed by all except the* THREE LORDS COMMISSIONERS *and* SECRETARY, *who remain in L. foreground, the* FELLOWS *in R. foreground, and* PENN, *who approaches the latter with a gay air.*

PENN. Why this trouble? Christ Church is a noble structure [*indicating it largely with his hands*], University College is a pleasant place, Magdalen College is a comely building. The walks are pleasant [*indicating them*], and it is convenient, just at the entrance to the city. Let the Romans have these, and, by my troth, they will ask no more!

DR. PUDSEY. We cannot!

> [PENN *shrugs his shoulders and goes off. The* COMMISSIONERS *approach the* FELLOWS, *as* HOUGH *and* FAIRFAX, *with* PORTER, LOCKSMITH, *and* UNDERGRADUATES, *also approach them from R.*

BP. OF CHESTER. Gentlemen, we are here to learn that you have elected the Bishop of Oxford, in obedience to the King's command.

DR. PUDSEY. Our conscience does not suffer us. Firstly—

BP. OF CHESTER. Aye! Aye!

DR. PUDSEY. By reason of the Statutes to which we are sworn!

BP. OF CHESTER. [*in disorder*] You are too bold! Know that, if you persist, we must here and now deprive you—

DR. PUDSEY. If it be the King's will.

C. JUSTICE. Yet, think!

FELLOWS. We are agreed and fixed.

BP. OF CHESTER. [*passionately*] Then, by the powers given us, we do expel you all! [*Taking the buttery book and a pen from his* SECRETARY *and striking a line through their names.*] You are deprived! Poor fools! For a word, a name, to give up your pleasant lodgings and your ample fare!

DR. PUDSEY. Aye, for a word—for conscience is a word! Yet I must protest.

DR. HOUGH. [*stepping to the front, through the* FELLOWS] And I—I do protest against your proceedings in prejudice of my rights and freehold, as all illegal, null, and void! And I do appeal to our Sovereign Lord the King in his Courts of Justice! [*The* UNDERGRADUATES, *&c. raise a loud hum of applause.*]

C. JUSTICE. This is a riot! Aye, by Heaven, it is near to treason! You, Sir, yield me instantly the keys of your lodge!

DR. HOUGH. I dare not!

C. JUSTICE. Porter! Give me the keys!

PORTER. I will not [*flings down his badge*].

C. JUSTICE. There is a locksmith! Bid him come!

LOCKSMITH. [*running off*] I am afraid!

C. JUSTICE. I will speedily set this to rights! If the civil power awe you not, there are soldiers! [*To his* SECRETARY] Send troopers hither!

> [*As the* SOLDIERS *enter slowly* (*L.*), *the* FELLOWS, *with upward looks at the College, or with bent and sorrowful heads, exchange affectionate greetings and farewells, as encouraging one another. Some support the steps of an aged* FELLOW, *one and another looking back as they prepare to go.*]

DR. SMITH. The King's will be done.

DR. HOUGH. Aye, so be it, if it must be! Come, all;
And in the Chapel we have served so long
We'll sing our last and saddest evensong!

> [*Exeunt* (*R.*), *the* FELLOWS *slowly, attended by mourning* UNDERGRADUATES, *the* COMMISSIONERS *and* SOLDIERS *following, after a slight interval. Chapel bell rings feebly.*]

Exeunt omnes.

STANLEY WEYMAN.

Plate XXXIII

DR. SAMUEL JOHNSON, d. 1784
From a picture at Trinity College.
(Oxf Hist. Portr. Exhn., 1906, No. 108.)

THE Revolution brought prosperity to England, to Oxford first disunion and then intellectual decay. The early sovereigns of the House of Hanover, whatever their merits, were not likely either to inspire high ideals or to encourage learning. Oxford, then as always an epitome of England, became rich and prosperous, idle and unlearned.

But learning and piety were not left without witness: Wesley and Johnson do something to redeem eighteenth-century Oxford from obscurity, and show that she had still in her, though it was dormant for a while, the spirit which was to show itself in the many 'movements' of the nineteenth century.

CARFAX IN THE EIGHTEENTH CENTURY

Otho Nicholson's Conduit, which supplied the city with water, is on the left.

A SCENE IN THE
EIGHTEENTH CENTURY

Circa A.D. 1785

THE scene represents the visit of King George III to Oxford in 1785. 'Farmer George,' as his people loved to call him, thoroughly understood the home life of Englishmen, and moved in and out among them with more simplicity than his Tudor and Stuart predecessors. Hence, the Oxford which he visits is one busy with its ordinary life and amusements. A fair, not unlike the St. Giles's Fair which makes Oxford lively in the first week of every September, is in full swing; jugglers and travelling shows are competing to amuse the people, while fine ladies and gentlemen condescend to take part in the popular gaiety. A mail coach drives up into the middle of the fair, full of those whose business or pleasure brings them to Oxford. Suddenly a running footman enters with the news that the King's barge is at hand, and as it approaches the royal party is greeted with Handel's Water Music. The King, who is accompanied by the Queen and six of his children—three princes and three princesses—with the Earl of Harcourt and his Countess, is met by the Vice-Chancellor, Proctors, and a deputation of the Heads of Houses. After the formal greeting, the royal party move through the fair. When the fun is once more at its height, the St. Frideswide music which opened the Pageant is heard in the distance, and the final scene shows us the successive groups which have represented the successive stages of Oxford's long history of a thousand years. Saints and scholars, Kings and

Courtiers, Friars and Townsfolk, Churchmen of the old form of faith and Churchmen of the new, Cavaliers and Puritans, all have played their part and helped to make Oxford what she now is.

Like 'the stuff that dreams are made of', they fade away; 'dressed in a little brief authority,' they served their generation, and in virtue of that service they still live.

> We men . . . must vanish; be it so!
> Enough, if something from our hands have power
> To live, and act, and serve the future hour;
> And if, as toward the silent tomb we go,
> Through love, through hope and faith's transcendent dower,
> We feel that we are greater than we know.

J. WELLS.

PLATE XXXV

DR JOHN RADCLIFFE
d. 1714

The well-known physician, and the most munificent benefactor to Oxford in the eighteenth century. The founder of the Radcliffe Infirmary, Observatory, and Library. From a picture by Sir G. Kneller, owned by Dr Radcliffe's Trustees (Oxf Hist Port John *4 5* No 223)

THE SECRET OF OXFORD

By 'Q'

'Up, up, my friends, and quit your books!'

ON Wednesday, June 26th (so my Oxford Almanack tells me) Bodley's Library closes its doors; and early next day the citizens and Oxford men in their generations turn out to disport themselves in Christ Church Meadows. It should be a great day. According to Whitaker, June 27th has already been made memorable by the peaceful death of a publisher (John Murray) and the hanging of an author (Dr. Dodd); but it may be said without disrespect to either of these events that if the promoters of the Oxford Pageant mean to start an epoch, one of the most eligible dates in the calendar remains open to them. Only, if they aspire to start it by divulging the secret of Oxford, I take leave to warn them—not regretfully—that they court disappointment.

Know you her secret none can utter?

—if I may quote one of the older bards. The secret, like every other immortal one, looks easy and lies open to anybody to attempt; while, like every other immortal one, it grows harder just as you begin to understand it. But the disguise which Oxford builds up in front of it ought not to delude even an American visitor for more than an hour or two. It consists in looking old. Precisely because her secret lies in youth, Oxford is pertinacious in whispering from her towers the last enchantment of the Middle Age, and even in supplying the decay of her old buildings with a frontage more mediaeval than the Middle Age itself. She exhibits chained books and claims an asset in the effect of her climate on friable stone. She carries the pretence to lengths that would be unfair if they were less naïvely fond.   You enter a college hall, and the portraits conspire to persuade you that Alma Mater suckles few children beneath the age of sixty.   Artless, primitive jest!

Although, in spite of the Court of King's Bench, King Alfred the Great did not found University, that eminent College, Oxford has undoubtedly lasted a long time.   But she is not therefore old, any more than Apollo and the Nine are old.   On the contrary she is immortally young.   Her quadrangles, her halls, her streets, her meadows, owe their unfading charm to the procession that has passed through them, and is still passing, of young faces, young voices, young hearts equally insatiate of the present and avid of the future.   J R Green, loyal son of City and University, was not far from the secret when he wrote: 'The charm of the place lies in a single difference from the world without it . . . Oxford is in truth neither historic, nor theological, nor academical.   It is simply young.'   A walk down the High (he said) tells more of the actual life of Oxford than all the books and treatises in the world.   'The first impression one receives is the true one; half the faces one meets are the faces of boys.'   So Froude was not far from the secret when, returning to Oxford after twenty-eight years' absence, he quoted happily Quevedo's happy allusion to the Tiber, 'The fugitive alone is permanent.'   Some drops of rain drove him to the Star Inn.—

'I sat and sipped my wine, thinking of the fate of cities—of Nineveh the renowned. . . . But a sunburst took place, the shower ceased, all became fresh and clear.   I saw several gownsmen pass down the street, and I sallied forth again.   Several who were in front of me, so full was I of old imaginings, I thought might be old friends whom I should recognize.   How idle!   I strolled to the Isis.   It was all glitter and gaiety.   The sun shone out warmly and covered the surface of the river with gold.   Numerous skiffs of the University men were alive on the water, realizing the lines,—

> Some lightly o'er the current swim,
> Some show their gaily gilded trim
>   Quick glancing to the sun.'

So again—to go back a couple of centuries—old Stephen Penton (although, according to Antony Wood, he had 'a rambling head') was not far from the secret, when in 1685, in a little book called *The Guardian's Instruction*, he told how with many misgivings he came up to enter his son at the University.

'After dinner I went to the public bowling-green, it being the only recreation I can affect. Coming in, I saw half-a-score of the finest youths the sun, I think, ever shined upon. They walked to and fro with their hands in their pockets to see a match played by some scholars and some gentlemen fam'd for their skill. I gaped also and stared as a man in his way would doe; but a country ruff gentleman, being like to lose, did swear at such a rate that my heart did grieve that those fine young men should hear it and know there was such a thing as swearing in the kingdom. Coming to my lodgings, I charged my son never to go to such publick places unless he resolved to quarrel with me.'

It is a far cry back from the Oxford of the seventeenth to the Oxford of the fourteenth, thirteenth, twelfth centuries; from the city of colleges and gardens where Charles I held his Court, to the filthy streets and crowded wooden tenements of a mediaeval University town, before Walter of Merton or William of Wykeham laid out their transforming examples. The directors of the Pageant may set the bells of St. Mary's and St. Martin's clashing one against another for the great riot of St. Scholastica's Day, 1354, and Mr. Godley himself may write the libretto; but even for those of us who have been privileged to take a modest part in a Town and Gown row, these alarums and excursions will scarcely carry our imagination across the gulf dividing the undergraduate of to-day and his early predecessors unless we keep hold on the changeless character of youth. The conditions are almost inconceivably different. We have, if we would go back to the beginning, to picture an Oxford in which only a few Jews' houses were built of stone; in which the herded students from all quarters of England, Scotland, Europe, had scarcely a recreation beyond drinking and dicing in taverns; where the upper windows discharged their slops into open gutters running midway down the alleys; where in cold weather (and it can be cold in Oxford) the lecturer talked foggily by lantern-light or within unglazed windows to a group of scholars blowing on their nails and shuffling their feet in the straw. Sunny Bologna glazed the windows of its University lecture-rooms with paper: but the lack of light in an Oxford Lecture-room, or for that matter in almost every English house, from September to May, must have been terrible; and it is only by bearing this and other winter discomforts in mind that we can understand in Chaucer and every early poet the ever-present sense of spring-time as an exchange of hell for heaven. With difficulty too, and certainly not with any help from a Pageant, can we picture to ourselves the extreme poverty in which many of the students lived who listened to Edmund Rich, Roger Bacon, Robert Grosseteste. Yet even the most famous story of their poverty ends on that note of youth which, if we hold to it, holds somewhere the secret of Oxford. There lodged together (we are told) three students so poor that they had but one *cappa* between them to cover their tunics: and so they took it in turns, the one going abroad in the *cappa* to lecture, while the other two kept their room. They fared on bread and porridge and a little wine, and never saw meat or fish but on Sundays and holy days: and yet the story winds up that Richard, of Chichester, who was one of the three, always remembered this time as the jolliest in his life—*et tamen saepe retulit quod nunquam in vita sua tam iucundam tam delectabilem duxerat vitam.* There, in brief apologue, shines the spirit of youth which is the spirit of Oxford.

But listen to another which, though perhaps unhistorical, seems to me yet more illustrative. In the days when the biretta (or mortar board) was the coveted badge of the Mastership in Arts, two very young Masters, having scraped up their pence to purchase the headgear, flaunted it together in a walk to Bagley Wood. Their names were Richard Hamond and Walter Treverbyn; and the day, though bright, was boisterous, with north-westerly squalls. On their way home across Folly Bridge a gust caught Hamond's biretta and blew it clean off his head into the river—*irreparabile damnum*, for he could not swim and had not a shilling to purchase another.

Treverbyn glanced at his friend's face. 'Of us two it is both or none,' said he, plucked off his own biretta, and sent it skimming into the flood. So they walked up St. Aldate's, sharing one another's humiliation, while the two hats danced in a bumping-race down the flood to Iffley.

In later years they married and lived remote from one another; which was lucky, for their wives could never, by any possibility, have agreed. Also they themselves took up very hotly with irreconcilable political opinions. Yet they died in the end having never entertained a thought of one another that was less than kind. For in the given hour, at Oxford, they had learnt the secret at the price of two Masters' caps; and though neither could ever explain the secret, it remained with them ineffaceably.

I say confidently, therefore, that the Historical Pageant of 1907 can never divulge the secret of Oxford. It may do better, though. Merely by being youthful, ardent, gay; by putting a spirit of life into its moving pictures; by dragging Antiquity to the meadows, to dance an hour for its juniors; it may pass into the secret itself and be of a piece with it.—

> Tower tall, city wall,
>   A river running past;
> Youth played when each was made,
>   And shall them all outlast.

A. T. QUILLER COUCH.

OFFICERS OF THE PAGEANT

AND

MEMBERS OF COMMITTEES

Master of the Pageant:

FRANK LASCELLES, Esq.

Stage Manager: JOHN DOUGLASS, Esq.

Assistant Stage Managers: Messrs. A. E. COURT, B. BARTON, and C. VERNON.

Master of the Music:

H. P. ALLEN, Esq., M.A., D.Mus.

Music Committee: J. VARLEY ROBERTS, Esq., D.Mus.; A. WIBLIN, Esq.;
H. B. WILSDON, Esq.

Master of the Robes

DION CLAYTON CALTHROP, Esq.

Artists: Messrs. J. BYAM SHAW, R.I., C. RICKETTS, J. R. SKELTON,
G. A. POWNALL; Misses ELEANOR FORTESCUE BRICKDALE,
MAUDE TINDAL ATKINSON, MARGARET FLETCHER, EVELYN
LOMAX.

Dramatic Authors:

LAURENCE HOUSMAN, Esq.
ROBERT BRIDGES, Esq., M.A., M.B.
LAURENCE BINYON, Esq., B.A.
C. OMAN, Esq., M.A., F.S.A., F.B.A.
A. D. GODLEY, Esq., M.A.

W. A. RALEIGH, Esq., M.A., D.Litt.
JAMES B. FAGAN, Esq.
Miss ELIZABETH WORDSWORTH,
Principal of Lady Margaret Hall.
STANLEY WEYMAN, Esq., B.A.

Special Advisers:

Dramatic: H. BEERBOHM TREE, Esq.; ARTHUR BOURCHIER, Esq., M.A.;
H. B. IRVING, Esq., M.A.; W. J. MORRIS, Esq., M.A.

Musical: Sir HUBERT PARRY, Bart., M.A., D.Mus., Hon. D.C.L., C.V.O.

Heraldry: Sir A. S. SCOTT-GATTY, F.S.A., C.V.O., Garter Principal King-
at-Arms.

Armour: The Rt. Hon. Viscount DILLON, M.A., F.S.A.

Ecclesiastical Vestments: Rev. F. E. BRIGHTMAN, M.A., Vice-President of
Magdalen College.

Academic and Civic Robes: F. MADAN, Esq., M.A., F.S.A.; JOSEPH
WELLS, Esq., M.A.

Honorary Secretaries:

Captain COULSON, J.P.

Councillor G. CLARIDGE DRUCE, Hon. M.A., Ex-Mayor of Oxford.

FINANCE COMMITTEE

The Right Worshipful the Mayor of Oxford (Councillor E. J. Brooks), *Chairman*.

The Deputy-Mayor of Oxford (Councillor Francis Twining), *Treasurer*.

The Sheriff of Oxford (Councillor S. Hutchins), *Vice-Chairman*.

AUDIT COMMITTEE

E. R. Bridson, Esq., 104 Woodstock Road, Oxford.

Stephen M. Burrows, Esq., M.A., Norham Gardens, Oxford.

M. N. Cotes, Esq., London and County Bank, 121 High Street, Oxford.

W. Margetts, Esq., Southfield House, Cowley Road, Oxford.

F. P. Morrell, Esq., M.A , J.P., Black Hall, Oxford.

Alderman J. H. Salter, J.P., Boar's Hill, Oxford.

Alderman Jason Saunders, J.P., The Cedars, Park Town, Oxford.

Montague W. Wootten-Wootten, Esq., J P., Headington, Oxon.

MASTERS OF CEREMONIES

W. F. Cooper, Esq. (*Chairman*), 83 High Street, Oxford.

Stephen M. Burrows, Esq., M.A., Norham Gardens, Oxford.

H. E. Counsell, Esq., F.R.C.S., 37 Broad Street, Oxford.

J. M. Eldridge, Esq., Bank Chambers, Oxford.

W. P. Ellis, Esq., M.D., Kidlington, Oxon.

Councillor W. E. Fayers, 12 Queen Street, Oxford.

G. Gardiner, Esq., 32 Beaumont Street, Oxford.

A. D. Godley, Esq., M.A., 4 Crick Road, Oxford.

Rev. J. Stuart Hay, B.A. (*Hon. Sec.*), 10 Oriel Street, Oxford.

R. Hitchings, Esq., M.R.C.S., 37 Holywell Street, Oxford.

H. P. Riley, Esq., 5 Chalfont Road, Oxford.

Captain R. S. Rowell, 115 High Street, Oxford.

Rev. E. F. Smith, M.A., 151 Banbury Road, Oxford.

CONSULTATIVE COMMITTEE

C. Oman, Esq., M.A., F.S.A., F.B.A. (*Chairman*), Chichele Professor of Modern History.

F. Madan, Esq., M.A., F.S.A., Sub-Librarian of the Bodleian (*Hon. Sec.*).

The Rt. Hon. Viscount Dillon, M.A., F.S.A., Curator of the Tower Armouries, Trustee of the British Museum, and of the National Portrait Gallery.

Cyril Bailey, Esq., M.A., Fellow and Tutor of Balliol.

C. Raymond Beazley, Esq., M.A., F.R.G.S., Sub-Warden of Merton.

Rev. F. E. Brightman, M.A., Vice-President of Magdalen.

Rev. Andrew Clark, M.A., LL.D., Hon. Fellow of Lincoln.

Arthur J. Evans, Esq., M.A., D.Litt., LL.D., F.R.S., F.S.A., F.B.A., Keeper of the Ashmolean.

C. H. Firth, Esq., M.A., LL.D., F.B.A., Regius Professor of Modern History.

A. D. Godley, Esq., M.A., Fellow and Tutor of Magdalen.

Rev. W. H. Hutton, M.A., B.D., Fellow and Tutor of St. John's.

J. A. R. Marriott, Esq., M.A., Sec. Oxford University Extension Delegacy.

John L. Myres, Esq., M.A., F.S.A., Student and Tutor of Christ Church.

R. Lane Poole, Esq., M.A., F.B.A., Fellow of Magdalen.

R. S. Rait, Esq., M.A., Fellow of New College, Secretary of the Oxford Historical Society.

W. A. Raleigh, Esq., M.A., D.Litt., Professor of English Literature.

Rev. Hastings Rashdall, M.A., D.Litt., Fellow and Tutor of New College.

C. Grant Robertson, Esq., M.A., Fellow of All Souls.

E. de Sélincourt, Esq., M.A., D.Litt., University Lecturer in Modern English Literature.

Rev. E. M. Walker, M.A., Fellow and Tutor of Queen's.

Joseph Wells, Esq., M.A., Fellow and Tutor of Wadham.

LADIES' GENERAL COMMITTEE

INCLUDING LEADERS OF EPISODES AND SECRETARIES

The Countess of Jersey.
The Viscountess Valentia.
The Lady Teignmouth.
The Lady Ottoline Morrell.
The Lady Margaret Watney.
The Mayoress of Oxford.
Lady Aitchison.
Lady Gray.
Lady O'Malley.
Lady Stainer.
Hon. Mrs. E. Ponsonby.
Miss Acland.
Mrs. Alington.
Mrs. Allen.
The Misses Anson.
The Misses Archer Houblon.
Mrs. Bevers.
Mrs. Blackwell.
Mrs. Bourne.
Mrs. A. J. Butler.
Mrs. Collier.
Mrs. Cook.
Mrs. F. Cooper.
Mrs. Coulson.
Mrs. Cunard.
Mrs. Daniel.
Mrs. Dodgson.
Mrs. Driver.
Mrs. Egerton.
Mrs. Firth.
Miss Fletcher.
Mrs. Furneaux.
Mrs. Furniss.
Mrs. Gallon.
Mrs. Gardiner.
Mrs. Gaskell.
Mrs. Godley, *Hon. Sec.*
Mrs. Gotch.

Miss Haig-Brown.
Mrs. Halford.
Miss Hardcastle.
Mrs. Hitchcock.
Miss Holman.
Mrs. S. Hutchins.
Mrs. Iliffe.
Mrs. Jackson.
Mrs. Lock.
Mrs. T. Lucas.
Mrs. Madan.
Mrs. Max Müller.
Mrs. F. P. Morrell.
Mrs. Muirhead.
Mrs. Oman.
Mrs. Ottley.
Mrs. Pope.
Miss Price.
Mrs. Prowse.
Mrs. Raleigh.
Mrs. Rashdall.
Miss F. Rawnsley.
Mrs. Rhŷs.
Mrs. T. H. Rose.
Mrs. Rowell.
Miss Sayers.
Mrs. R. Smith.
Miss Swann.
Miss Symonds.
Mrs. R. Thomas.
Mrs. F. Twining.
Mrs. G. E. Underhill, *Hon. Sec.*
Mrs. Vernon.
Mrs. E. Warren.
Mrs. Whitmarsh.
Mrs. Whittington.
Mrs. J. Wicks.
Miss Wordsworth.

Mrs. Wykeham.

AMPHITHEATRE COMMITTEE

W. P. Ellis, Esq., M.D. (*Chairman*), Kidlington, Oxon.

Councillor S. M. Acott, 124 High Street, Oxford.

Alderman F. W. Ansell, 99 Banbury Road, Oxford.

G. E. Baker, Esq., M.A., 74 Banbury Road, Oxford.

Councillor Surgeon-General Bradshaw, Hon. M.A., C.B, K.H.P., 111 Banbury Road, Oxford.

J. T. Filsell, Esq., 48 Banbury Road, Oxford.

G. Gardiner, Esq., 32 Beaumont Street, Oxford.

The Sheriff (Councillor S. Hutchins), 157 Woodstock Road, Oxford.

Councillor H. S. Kingerlee, 102 Woodstock Road, Oxford.

E. Knowles, Esq., 36 Holywell Street, Oxford.

C. Rippon, Esq., Editor *Oxford Times*, 11 New Road, Oxford.

Councillor C. M. Taphouse, 3 Magdalen Street, Oxford.

R. Thomas, Esq., 32 Lonsdale Road, Oxford.

V. H. Veley, Esq, M.A., D.Sc., F.R.S., 20 Bradmore Road, Oxford.

Colonel S. Waller, C V.O., 28 Bardwell Road, Oxford.

♣

PRESS COMMITTEE

C. W. Floriday, Esq., 162 Walton Street, Oxford.

Claude Moore, Esq., B.A., Bairdown, Woodstock Road, Oxford.

W. J. Morris, Esq., M.A., Farthinghoe, Brackley.

H. S. Puttick, Esq., 223 Cowley Road, Oxford.

J. G. Radcliffe, Esq., St. Aldate's, Oxford.

H. M. Turner, Esq, 4 The Turl, Oxford.

A. Tyler, Esq., Leopold Street, Oxford.

Councillor C. Vincent, 3 Polstead Road, Oxford.

PERFORMERS' COMMITTEE

Councillor S. M. Acott (*Chairman*), 124 High Street, Oxford.
Capt. A. A. Bridgewater, Drill Hall, St. Cross Road, Oxford.
W. F. Cooper, Esq., 83 High Street, Oxford.
Capt. B. V. Darbishire, M.A., 202 Iffley Road, Oxford.
F. Dearle, Esq., c/o Messrs. Goold, 3 Queen Street, Oxford.
R. Evans, Esq., 11 Warnborough Road, Oxford.
Councillor W. E. Fayers, 12 Queen Street, Oxford.
C. W. Floriday, Esq , 162 Walton Street, Oxford.
T. E. Foort, Esq., 266 Iffley Road, Oxford.
J. Gynes, Esq., 16 Cowley Road, Oxford.
W. Harris, Esq. (Messrs. Acott & Co.), 124 High Street, Oxford.
G. H. Heath, Esq., 5 Parks Road, Oxford.
Lt.-Col. Aylmer Jones, 252 Iffley Road, Oxford.
Councillor H. Lewis, 125 Woodstock Road, Oxford.
E. Linaker, Esq., Editor *Oxford Chronicle*, 119 High Street, Oxford.
Councillor J. B. Lucas, Sunnyside, 66 Botley Road, Oxford.
Claude Moore, Esq., Bairdown, Woodstock Road, Oxford.
H. Parsons, Esq., 3 Church Villas, Cowley Road, Oxford.
H. S. Puttick, Esq., 223 Cowley Road, Oxford.
Capt. R. S. Rowell, 115 High Street, Oxford.
Councillor W. Turrill, Oakthorpe, Woodstock Road, Oxford.
E. Twining, Esq., 4 Lonsdale Road, Oxford.
Councillor C. Vincent, 3 Polstead Road, Oxford.
Councillor F. F. Vincent, 94 High Street, Oxford.
Alderman H. W. W. Woodward, 51 Cornmarket Street, Oxford.

HORSE COMMITTEE

Councillor J. Hastings (*Chairman*), 14 Polstead Road, Oxford.

H. J. Fletcher, Esq. (*Master of the Horse*), Wolvercote, Oxon.

W. Brain, Esq., Kidlington, Oxon.

Captain A. A. Bridgewater, Drill Hall, St. Cross Road, Oxford.

R. Butterfield, Esq., 12 New Road, Oxford.

W. F. Cooper, Esq., 83 High Street, Oxford.

Roy Downing, Esq., 10 Park Crescent, Oxford.

F. M. Gask, Esq., Northleigh, Oxon.

F. Gillard, Esq., George Hotel, Cornmarket Street, Oxford.

Sergt.-Major J. L. Goldie, St. Thomas's House, Paradise Street, Oxford.

G. T. Jones, Esq., 35 St. Margaret's Road, Oxford.

Squadron Sergt.-Major A. E. Puttick, Woodstock.

J. Rhodes, Esq., Lamb and Flag Hotel, St. Giles's, Oxford.

Captain R. S. Rowell, 115 High Street, Oxford.

F. Ryman-Hall, Esq., J.P., Summerhill, Summertown, Oxford.

Alderman Jason Saunders, J P., The Cedars, Park Town, Oxford.

Dr. M. Sherwood, 17 Beaumont Street, Oxford.

A. E. Simmons, Esq., Sandford, Oxon.

Rev. E. F. Smith, M.A., 151 Banbury Road, Oxford.

C. Taylor, Esq., Ascot Manor, Wallingford.

H. M. Turner, Esq., 4 The Turl, Oxford.

R. J. Verney, Esq., M.R.C.V.S., 23 Beaumont Street, Oxford.

Lightning Source UK Ltd.
Milton Keynes UK
UKHW020634060223
416537UK00012B/2679

9 781376 706024